The Mystic and the Pig Thief

FRAN LOCK is a sometime itinerant dog whisperer and poet, now living and working in London. Her debut collection *Flatrock* (Little Episodes) was launched in May 2011. Her work has appeared in various places, including *Ambit*, *Poetry London*, *The Stinging Fly*, and in *Best British Poetry* 2012 (Salt). She is the winner of the 2014 *Ambit* Poetry Competition.

Also by Fran Lock

Flatrock (Little Episodes, 2011)

The Mystic
and the Pig Thief

FRAN LOCK

SALT

CROMER

PUBLISHED BY SALT PUBLISHING
12 Norwich Road, Cromer, Norfolk NR27 0AX United Kingdom

© Fran Lock, 2014

The right of Fran Lock to be identified as the
author of this work has been asserted by her in accordance
with Section 77 of the Copyright, Designs and Patents Act 1988.

Salt Publishing 2014

Printed and bound in the United Kingdom by Lightning Source UK Ltd

Typeset in Swift 9.5 / 13

ISBN 978 1 907773 70 9 paperback

1 3 5 7 9 8 6 4 2

For Pig Thief and for Marty, journey well.

Contents

Acknowledgments

Some of these poems first appeared in *Blackbox Manifold*, *Lung Jazz: Young British Poets for Oxfam* (Cinnamon Press, 2012), *Poetry London*, *Poems in Which*, *Best British Poetry 2012* (Salt, 2012) and *The Stinging Fly*.

I'd like to thank Roddy Lumsden's Wednesday group for their advice and their encouragement, and my fellow toilers in obscurity for their years of unstinting friendship and poetry-related support.

My warmest thanks to Steev Burgess and my cousin Jack Varnell, for helping me in more ways than they'll ever know, and to Roddy Lumsden, for his perception and his patience.

My solidarity and my love to The Clan, to The Tribe, and to my long-suffering husband; to His Royal Kidderness, Chief Unicorn, Feminism in General, and to The Court of Dogs.

But most of all to 'Pig Thief', journey well.

The Mystic and the Pig Thief

How I met your father

They couldn't teach me anything:
those temperant aunties, patient
as potato starch,
wringing their thrift with both hands.
All shoestring and broomsticks,
alive, alive oh.

I was for War Games and boys.
Bitch, with my glitterbug predilections.
Minnowy slither, I shimmied pink,
a tickled trout.

I was for tavern agro, the slant
baksheesh of some midlife herbsman:
come away, he says, his tash
whisking my arms like drum-
brushes patterning jazz. Oh,
we was high, we was mighty;
my eyes done kohl as big and black
and flat as welders' goggles.

Couldn't teach me anything:
in heels I clatter like a one man band
and my hair vamped into black rattails;
my nails are sassy plectrums. I gliss him
a relish of kisses, glad scavenger in biker
boots, and micro-mini like a fuckin' tide mark.

He was a gruff alumnus for hardtime,
a baleful operative with scanty vocab
and a sentimental love of Country.

I put on my posh togs and sucked him
in his solvent abuse and Brit-bruised flesh.
I kissed him in his cop-kills and carcinogens;
I lay in his patent-leather lap and drank him up,
all thirsty sulphides.

Beyond hope, they said. I learnt
instead the ragged plainsong
of prison visitation; the tinkling
sleighbell vitriol of public telephones.
I learnt the well-versed tortoiseshell
of men who bear their beatings,
and the jagged, jet-lagged barter
of meetings chopped by mesh.

And I grew you. In the conjugal
kitchen sink of my own self.
You, scratching like a lab rat,
a tiny bone clinker; a mean little jinx
shifting your drum-dance, making
me mad with your snide poltergeisting.

Girl, I flummoxed and spiralled and
cursed him and spat!

Couldn't teach me anything.
Or him, straggled now, a sullen codger
in the lapse of his leanness.
Only you, child, a tender swell
like an abscess on a tooth.
It's you who go to get learning done.

I wouldn't let them come at me
with knuckles and suction. I tore up
and off and you, flightless namesake,
rounding me out like an echo.

Timely tomboy,
look at you now.
I'm this close to dancing.

Circus barker

Pinioned, amphibious,
they peg out the tent and put
a slit in its rubberised belly.
This cut opens like a cat's mouth,
crude λ revealing red, revealing
sawdust, used tissues, dung.
These are Circus Humours.
These are the Cartwheel Workings
of God, that pious organ grinder. Roll up,
roll up for the burnt-blood smell of popcorn;
candyfloss fuzzed between rotary blades.

My name is
Pleased to Meet You.
I fold up small
like a boy
in a basket of knives.
Neat Sisyphus, I roll
a round, red ball.
My name is
Go, Dog Go!
I fold up small.

They make a circle of salted earth
and sieve the light through high
wires, preachy as pylons,
nooses looping the frosted air.
And these wires catch at birds:
petite baroque in tight white Lycra.
Birds go slamming at the safety
net, a catchall crotch, at the dizzy
floor, the centre partings of the parents.
Light as an empty egg-box, birds,
light like the mummified corpses of mice.

My name is
Upside-down Frown.
I caper.
I wear the conical hat
of a dunce.
I snaffle and goof
in a paper ruff.
My name is
Old King Cole.
I caper.

They rig up a nag with a chin strap.
In the *any old iron!* of the night
watch her lunge and drum, gaga
as glue. And I am flea-bit,
madder than the English.
Bears are oligarchs, drunken in sway,
And scruff-doves marble silk with shit.
Doves are the ghosts of dead costumes.

They've got to crew-up with toothless
loonies, Glasgow smiles all painted
on with red wax. Old dossers to gush
and honk and throw paper fire. The job
of the crowd is to writhe as if burning.

My name is
Teacher's Pet.
Stroke me soft.
My name is
The Great Satan.
Count my teeth.
My name is
Sneaky Pete.

[5]

A future-proof
philosopher.
Stroke me soft
as bearded ladies.
Harlequin.
My nose is wet.

The Dangerous Dogs Act

The pit bull puts his chin on the table, mute
as a hog-roast. These dogs, with their noses
slick like the bellies of Colorado River toads,
will split the wrist below the brittle radius.
To them all men are mere devilled kidney, creamed
polenta, cracked black pepper; they'd pop your tasty
scaphoid like a Cajun navy bean. Their eyes are red-
rimmed, stoner-wide, and they are always hungry.
Just weigh the smooth crocodile credentials
of that locked and loaded jaw. Pure Wookey Hole!
Oh, the *ivory towers* of their teething trouble,
mouths like spooky grottoes. Don't you like them?

I watch you, *baby*, watching the black
tyre tread of their twitching lips, inner
tube tongues. They open slowly, moist,
like wet umbrellas. Aren't they lovely?
This yawning unfolds them, and you
are afraid, cupping your cock like a glass
slipper, scraping your chair on the scratch-
resistant laminate. I fondle the soft lapels
of *cloth ears,* rub crop circles into haunch
and flank. They won't bite, unless I tell them to.

Dear boy, I am The Dog Mother. I gesture
like a temptress and they follow my titbit
beck, snuffle for crumbs. Feral beldam,
I sit cross-legged in baskets. I speak
in a rough dog voice. My words are splintery
wishbones. I am The Dog Mother. You cannot
see it, but I have the head of a wolf and a skew-
whiff bristle of hackles. This is my house: the spilled
milk smell of a recent whelping;
the coyote's hiccupping ringtone laugh, on
and on, like a slow dance, a druggy torch song.

Just so stories for dogs

Contrary to popular belief,
not everybody wants to be a cat.
Like all deposed tyrants
they are fanatical and bitter;
Holocaust deniers, reliving
their own small Nuremburgs daily.

Cats are cultists, petty, pampered
Crowleys, dabbling in sacrifice.
They carry mutilated birds
to the shrine of their own self-love.

Cats are haughty and perverse,
Dennis Wheatley Satanists, incestuous
aristos. They are believers in Blavatsky,
hereditary peerage and positive eugenics.

Cats are sentimental, *Völkisch,*
into blood and soil. They go about
building Jerusalem with their black
shirt scruples on, minor Mosleys all.

For dogs it is different.
We're less like only children.
Cooperation is important,
it's how we survive the winter.
Yes, I'd say I *was* a socialist.

Policemen are cats,
throwing their weight around
like impotent djinns.

Politicians are cats,
as pompous and ceremonial
as a bishop's tall hat.

Many people are cats.
You can tell a cat by its flat
face, a mask made out of a
paper plate.

Being a dog is intelligence work.
The humans might think I am sleeping,
curled up tight as a dead wasp, but no –

I am watching and waiting.
I know who all the cats are.
I have committed their names
to memory.

Human whispering

Mother's two legs too long to tuck
under herself like a frozen chicken.
Mother can't get small enough
to satisfy this sadness, this stalking
sense of *having failed*.

Mother isn't dainty. Too healthy
to be sad; blunt as the bloody
minded Bronze Age. Her body
succumbs to its own hopeless
weather nonetheless. She swears
oaths and kicks crap to cover her traces.
I want to disappear is something humans say.

My job is to make life better. I do this
by being brilliant: a firm little loaf
that fires at will. Just look at the trimmed
curly crust of my tail! Look how I line
up my teeths for inspection! I find them
neat and soldierly. I am pleased. I wag
my dense yellow body and sing *Hakuna
Matata*. This makes Mother smile.

Me and Mother understand each other.
I know her secret, how really she is
wild, a buckshot Alpha, clanking
with a pedigree of wounds.

Not a handbag human, not *ladylike*.
Her spread legs are a catapult's
ravenous Y. She has bone
splitting motives, she eats
her hapless mates. And yet,
she keeps me safe.

You see, she is morbid and specific
for survival. She can walk on ice;
she is beady eyed and rough,
well-travelled and always hungry.

She cries in crouch position, though,
more often now, since she became
captive, not domesticated. Broken
is not tame.

Poem in which I entertain a little fuchsia of the mind

Henry Joseph Darger is petrochemically skittish.
My pallet tends toward burnt toast. I wear a lot
of black and trail about the small hours, forlornly
psychedelic, stoned on a lowercase madness,
chewing the ends of my hair. But still, there are days
when the brain is adamant upon cabaret abstractions,
when thought is acutely botanical, and I quake to show
my shoved face before God.

Darger is deterrent. Every so often a friend will ferret
out, from the stark annals of psychosis, a cautionary looner.
The moral of their story's always *there but for the grace,* yet
still I insist, in my own world, on the credulous enriching
of the real. I tolerate the contingent universe with a bare
minimum of aggrieved benevolence. This is my mode
of life. No one will convince me that the dead don't walk.

It does scare me. It scares me mewling and raw
sometimes, to be a scraped complainant, stung
into whoops and cries, or the brain is some
excruciated garden, bawdy and histrionic
with flowers. I can't always stomach my own
bedraggled abundance.

But I would not give it up, even if
monsters snuck in the night and broke
my pinky fingers one by one; even if those six
beheading skellymen came and dragged at me
with teeth. I would carry on, gather up
my artillery curios, make my war face, fight.

Because I *am* a Vivian Girl, despite my gothy
deadpan. I am a rosy Shirley Temple with holy
medals and soldierly peccadilloes, my head
a swarm of curls.

In Abbieannia the fuchsias are chandeliering,
spooky and awkward; desolated gentians
drop their tragedian masks, and a winged
serpent stretches out the long, red blooper reel
of his body to bask in the snatching sun.

I draw back the curtains.
Darger proliferates nudities.

SM1 Suite

In the shrink-wrapped cotton
mouth of the day, I rise
with the ripe haze of fat-
fried grime and petrol. I descry
an illiterate *I Ching*: scattered
Kentucky like yarrow, greasing
its cryptic hexagrams.

Dog turds are gilding the curbs
in elaborate, studded turbans.
My new boots creak like sick beds,
my scatter-gun smattering of local
parlay might not be enough to get
me to the station, on time, intact:
Bitch, I'll faaking caat you!

The housing estate has made
a specialty of barking. The cash
converts are rocking up
to pawn their party favours.
This is Monday.

I am off to work, to flay
tight smiles in fitted kitchens;
mind my manners, grind my teeth
at denimed DILFs backing out
of sainted, shingle driveways.

I am gone to salt
my small talk with the mothers,
watch them tarting-up
in full length mirrors.
Faux celebs, collagen
and glossy combat. They count
out my cash and ask about my weekend.

I am gone to make nice
with teenage kid-hordes.
Abercrombied, fat happy-
slaparazzi, mobiling
each other for viral posterity.
Modern primitives in the lounge
of their leisurewear, get in my face
but I won't buy them cigarettes or cider.
We are not on the same side.

Mine is missionary. Mine
is to archive canine shapes
in grit flurries up the Mad Mile,
then flee, back to the dreggy
edge of town, my circuitry
skinned to the raw bravura
of domestic service and self-loathing.

Mine is the mastiff's Moby Dick back
glinting chivvied pewter.
Mine are yellow fiend-eyes,
Midwich-gold like curdled sun.
Mine, the Big Mac macho bulks,
of pit bull terriers, sleeking.

Sutton, in the second-
hand smoke of your morning,
cough me a gospel. I will grow wings,
a *slum-dog* apostle.
This is my church. This is my church.

II

Listen, a train passing under a bridge,
rocking us both with a pious shudder.
It is here that we come to skim
choice kisses, fat from cream.

It is here that in years to come,
the dirtpale men will find
a ration of skirmished bone,
small ribs, frail
as the dewclaws of dogs;
vertebrae littered
like mismatched cufflinks.

Adroit and desirous by night, wearing
our bold, black outlines, we're cartoons.
It is here we have come to marvel and char.
The town lit up by fire: defective
affinity, clownish, cultish monkey-love.

In years to come the scrubdirt men
will loot the ashblack earth, rooting
for relevant scraps. They will
scope our bodies, grimed in
their fumbling gridlock; gauche
polyblends warped to skanky ribbons.

But we will be beyond them.
Our scutty remains will reek like sulphur.

III

Ireland, pale and incredulous
in her mornings and her monasteries,
practised in a rustic catalepsy
that's more than sleep, but less
than death. It aches. I ache
like a Strad scraped into music.

Even though I straighten my hair
and read *The Guardian*, and you
are long since slogging-lost, gone
to catch crabs in the jaundiced North,
it sings like a chip pan fire in me.

God! I stretch my fingers to the sea:
come meet me in the shivering
ballistics of my loss. I haven't learnt
to live here. I am lavish and mournful
and good with my hands. Batshit mad.
A tribal snide. An egg-suck Garbo
in a black armband. My grief
is a fascist and it *vaants to be alone.*

Ireland, green as hospital
grade soap, where you struck poses,
russet-coloured, lamb-chop lean.
The bells in their tone-deaf dingdong;
stray dogs humping in the lumpy,
fuzzy dusk. It aches. I ache. The heart
expands like a frozen pipe.

And I round my vowels and read
The Guardian, look both ways
before crossing the street. I lock
my door and have bad dreams.
I live here now. Didn't I do well?

On this day in history

April 8, 2013

You was cooked in clay, my love,
and bursting like a chestnut. I saw
you threshed in heat, critter-
clenched; a spurting fist. I saw
your gashed mitten creak,
      blinking off
a loose caboodle of spikes.

Old men jabbed you with a stick,
spiteful pikers, poking.
You leaked curds, unravelled
in the mouth like string. I saw
you give 'em pangs, a bee-
sting pharmacopoeia
of small, twinging spines.

Pear-shaped captive.
Bed of nails. Eating you
was being Brer Rabbit
in the briar patch.
You was an artillery,
you tampered the tongue.

This dream returns;
I will return to you, not her,
some dead dyed-in-the-wool,
soiling herself at The Ritz.
April the 8th is Hedgehog day!

Tatty said it wouldn't kill me,
kiss of hot fat, the sad frisson
of a penance. Brothers ringing
bells for you, I thought, while I
crouched small behind tall
nettles, fingers down my throat.

Poem in which I gouge out his eyes with a soup spoon

A glorious Morticia,
my lips a study
in sense of occasion.
I spread my off-
white body above him,
soft as mosquito netting.

Chemically treated,
abundantly cunning.
I do not brandish,
but grasp like a nettle.
I want to cut him
as a diamond cuts glass;
bounce his head
off every curb
from Bogside to Brixton.

But here is a better idea,
an etiquette of scraping.
The spoon is sanitary and deaf,
Spaghetti Western Silver.

He lolls in lotus-eating cosh.
My punches do not wake him.
Green fingered as a gardener,
I begin my ministrations.

It isn't that I hate him.
But God,
that ornamental pedantry!
His Magdalen drawl!
His fish-eating sneer!
Can I really not tell
demitasse from *parfait*?

And how he made
his making love
an act of gap year heroism.
A fatuous Samaritan,
who condescends to fuck me.

I grew tired of being patronised,
dispensing hand-wash mercies
for the dry clean only care
of his Old Etonian ego.

A glorious Morticia, I draw
on gloves like a sawbones.
And smiling, with barbarian
gusto, I scoop to conquer.

Next bed but one

A banker's son, enriched
in Argyll socks. He snatches
handfuls of this heatwave,
stuffs them in his mouth,
in his pockets, up his shirt.
He's convinced the House
of Lords are Satan's Slaves.
He's drawn a face on top
of his face with a thick, red
felt tip pen.

Duty Nurse undresses him.
He viewfinds with his hands.
I fit into this Kodak moment.
His name is Eliot. He's not keen
on High Court judges either:
mummified figments in Viennetta
wigs, they want to steal the skins
of *all* Oxford Undergraduates. Not just
him. The sun is abhorrent to them,
he says. She gets him into his gown:
frat boy dressed for toga party.

I give Duty Nurse a look.
She pretends not to see.
Fine. Be like that. That doolally
moo-cow, Heather, is breast-
feeding a two litre Lucozade bottle.
Her nipples are long pipettes. Christ,
anyone can see that I am the least crazy
person here.

Occasionally there are visitors.
They stand about doing three
part harmonies, like girl groups
from the sixties. At night, we shift
for ourselves:

Heather, her bulk
like a Bedford, rocking
her reinforced bed; Eliot,
a cod Jack Frost, up against
the little plastic pane in the door,
trying to write his name in his breath.

The others are site machinery.
They list and creak. It is a kind
of spooky boredom. I want to get
gone, at the very least to be correctly
categorized as one of the Pouty Mad.
I shouldn't be here, watching
the chronically lopsided dodge
the meds and do their cringe-
worthy Imagineering.

I shouldn't be here among the women's magazines,
food in freeze-dried splinters, instant muck, bottles
of whey protein, chocolate slop to keep our *strength up.*

I tell myself I'm on some NASA training jag,
moon-walking through the secure ward's zero
g. Or I'm scuttled in a bunker, ducking fallout.
I count to fifty, fifty times, and close my eyes
and maybe, when the dust settles, a couple of us
will grope clear. Eliot and I, staggering cannibal,
mutant loons with eyes like wolves.

These thoughts do not comfort me. Outside, the only sky I can see is the colour of canned peaches. The world *may* have ended, as far as I know.

The erotic life of Michael Cochrane, stargazer

In the blue-collar catchments
of stone-clad catholic cul-de-sacs
the horse-doctored prodigies are high
on hand-spans of freebased fire.

Jobless oddments, skilled
in the unarmed combat of beat combos,
all bruised egos and bass guitars.

Lanky cadgers after
cigarettes on corners,
the gobby lords of mob rule
have the freedom of the city.
They chant their scatologies
into dim last-orders hours.

They gather liabilities of small change,
glut the skinned vision with dreggy nectar;
tricky-cheap libidinies of snow-blind powder.

They are buzzed. They are vexed.
They map the gashy dazzle of the stars,
webbing lush smoke to a rare near-heaven.

Radiant petechiae!
Fag burn in shop-lifted Saint-Laurent black!
The sacked thread-count of an inner-city sky!

It's beautiful –
beauty . . . fell . . .

His sign language slurs,
fogging acknowledgement into bliss.

Michael Cochrane gets his cock out,
hyphenates himself to the pulsing,
purple night with one sprigged, white morsel.

All the girls are long in limping love with him:
smiling like horses
with smeared peanut-
butter gums.

All the girls are long in lead-lined love with him:
drum-tight with lust they ache
to feather-bed on butter-blond
curds of fleece;
to lap his public laurels
with obscene and kittenish thirst.

All the girls' mothers
cannot hear themselves think
above the synced ticking
of their biological clocks,
their wombs rattle like kitchen sinks.

Michael Cochrane runs wild.
He is wide with tales of amateur stabbings.
He has the authority of a head wound!

He picks up chatty girlies,
all fan-psyche and cos-play;
humid beneath their pleats and gym knickers,
lurid as an Indian summer.

He strums to them.
Their fathers are the cronies
of civic improvement.

Girls with the names
of prohibition-era townships:
Mercy and Hope and Creed.

They map the gashy dazzle of the stars!
So drunk their breath lacquers the air:

There is no God, only what shines . . .
this is the belt . . . this is the bear . . .
this is the huntress . . . this is the angel . . .

This is the brain,
soft as beer-battered cod.
This is the literal dinge of a wasted life.

Michael Cochrane reeling.
Sunday's sewn up tight.
His remorse engorges, marrowfat.

In the blue-collared bottlenecks of brickbaffled towns,
medicated Gullivers are gearing up for odysseys.

Michael Cochrane talks stars, talks crazy catholic faff.
He fidgets with the women in the close-knit night.
He dwells on distant, deep-space things.
He has sharpened his longing, filing its teeth.

Daddus

And he has handed His Kingdom on: a world
of sturdy hurts, where Christ is a poleaxed
crock of saintliness, stooped in accentuant
moonlight, dancing down the obsolescent
eyries of *Shank* or *Turf*, piping ditties
to pious tribulation. He was an apostle, one
among many credulous sectmen, men with long
beards and narrow shoulders. He was from
a race of stark gonks, gurning furies, fucking
agog for The Lord, for the Light of The Lord,
waiting for the Lobotomising Light of The Lord
to ethnically cleanse them. Pogrom purists!
I have hated their dread handiwork long time.
Understand, he was a disciple, lethal groupie,
groomed in his own cold sweat, nights spent
drenched in obedient blotto: the wine, the blood,
the impeccable mercies of glowering priests.
Oh, how he clamoured for the crude largess
of Mother Church, his pink-white myxy eyes
fried in light like rotten scallops. An old
soak, greasing his guesswork with whiskey
and pills, kneading his guilt to a lump sum
like a payday loan, a sorry wad of misaffection.
He has passed this on: faith and other luminary
rackets, God as an eavesdropping slob who does
not love us. Heirs to this, come clutching
our Christian bygones, loud in the cry-wolf
chorus of our complaint; full of faint praise
and hashtag emptiness, an avatar bonanza
of national pride. Or we become loafing
minors, alibi scallies, hallooing the night.
Peek-a-boo pilgrims with indigo zits, an ape-
faced argument for Tory Borstal, *biggin' it
up* in the swank of our inbred beefing. Drab
children, grudging psychos, a demobbed

affront to the future, exhausting our outbursts
again. And he has handed on His Kingdom:
a raw quandary of body parts, *history*
in place of prayer. Us, his pop-eyed
progeny, bad to the bone in the deep-fried
faulty heat of summer, The North in a nutjob
ecstasy of crowd control, poxy with coppers.
And the stars are pale as grease spots, the cars
burn, our anger dissolves into shoddy barking.
We cling together, sing up for his commie hobres,
mummified amigos dispensing their old firebrand
benisons; we sing through the scurvy fuzz on
our tongues, sing a treasury of horrors.
It is our function. Skinned like him
to our nightcapped nerves. It never ends.
Pour it into proper nouns, acronyms, spirited
gigabyte drivel. A terrible poem that pushes
its luck. Hand it on, this way, for you, *Daddus*.

Bette Divis, fragments from her final (madhouse) interview

Ruth Elizabeth 'Bette' Davis was an American actress, principally of the late 1930s, noted for her willingness to take on unsympathetic roles. 'Hollywood always wanted me to be pretty' she once said, 'but I fought for realism'.

The Divis Flats (now demolished) were a working-class area of West Belfast in Northern Ireland, considered a 'flash point' during the height of the Troubles.

Bette Divis is a notorious cabaret performer. She may or may not be real.

I

I rave and have coarse manners.
My ingenious hair will trap you,
ravel you down to wincing fathoms.

Gaunt extremist, I
am no delicate comrade
but a mad bitch who takes
a fancy to nails while shrieking.

Marie Claire described my ribs
as seen through a thin, black blouse
as the slats of a Venetian blind.

I have a large eye and a short fuse.
I will shock you to your smart-
mouthed monosyllables. I sit,
suction-cupping smiles. I am not whole
in the way that supermodels are not whole.

I am jealous. I resent this world
like a cat resents a wicker cage. I spit
and you finish my sentences for me.
Lemon-scented English shits. I'm sharp
to you. Plantagenet pig-fuckers. Pedigrees.
Experts. I see you strut your semi-
detachments. Purse your lips. Peck at air.

II

My fingers and toes are crusty
with ten-carat hobnails; a blood-
red bantam shrapnel of rubies.
I gleam to my sea-leagued innards
as mermaids are said to do. But *cash
poor* skint to my split ends, lend us
a tenner. I'll put on dark glasses
to gloat with. My horse, with the saints
is marching in . . .

III

Resplendent in maiden-voyage,
exquisite as a forgery. I spread
my palms like a spirit medium . . .

My kisses bite the heads off bats
and gather nettles under bridges.
My kisses go collecting
sharpness like an axe head . . .

Fairest of them all and three-
sheets in stacked heels. Cracked
in the crypt of my spy-
craft, rocking. Tender
as tree huggers, dumb
as a bust of Beethoven.
I polish my plainsong.
The night belongs
to the lewd war effort of women . . .

Back-firing cars scatter their smokers' coughs.
Young love is for prominent corpses, dressed
in their Civil War best. This silence threads needles,
turns pages, makes blind as well as deaf . . .

There is nobody out there. Quiet
as a kitchen cupboard, the clinic
is putting its Petri dishes to bed. It isn't
in translation things are lost. I know
my place. I can't stop scratching. I strip
as bare as a bedsit bulb.
Golden as Good Housekeeping with all
my freshly laundered forward planning
on display. I drop aitches, stand in a corner
and shake like a fool . . .

I am Sista Inquisitionista
in my semblance medievalry.
Black Ray-Bans reclassify
my primping skull as *implement.*
Otherwise I'm naked, white
as deliquescent lye. I do not
scrub floors. I *don't.* I am very friendly . . .

This is a conditioned response.
More spittle than Pavlov. The world
retracts its witness statements. Silence
as a form of substance abuse. So dark
in the backs of limousines, at the bottom
of heart-shaped bathtubs. A size sixteen
with a lot to learn. I am ready for my close-up . . .

IV

A tournament mademoiselle, all peroxide and prime numbers.
You'll always do what she wants you to do. Not because you love
her, but because she profanes a frown with black lipstick. And
such glittering amputations! Derry's skyline sliding by like broken
fingernails! A wary Christmas of lights that haven't learned not to
mean emergency. Glum tackiness in spades and you, gazumped by
a Peter Pan collar and canvas pumps! It's too much! High fidelity
flapper in semi-permanent war paint. Fabulous. Simply fabulous . . .

Yes, I'll tell you about her. Bette is a bird
in her transgendered feather-light. Pulls
on her politic softness like a hunter's hood,
becomes religious and peeping. Picks
at berries, pits her wits. A flexy errand
girl. Her wings, in sentimental papershred,
are snowing like a pillow fight, white on
cotton gobbed, cat-got white . . .

Bette is a glassy eyed pinhead;
gimmicky-thin. A foxy kelpto
with hennaed hair. Eighth-weighing
wraith, chatting extravagant Hamlet
into the grumpy, scutty dusk
of Cardboard Belfast. Her kingdom
for a horse . . .

[34]

Bette is a cardamom scented
tough, a snapper-out-of trances.
Crouches like a roo baby, her face
is glossed by crying. A full tea
ceremony of tears. Fool proof pack
animal, she played outdoors in dirty
rags, goes stiff as a lancet when anybody
touches her. Her best defence
is a leper's rejoinder. She plaits her hair
and lights up the names of dead.
Her repercussions cluck and all she wants
is to bite the hand that feeds her . . .

Bette is as tall as a man. They say
she is *edgy* on stage. A provocative
mantis. A razor's compliment
of elbows. Shin-sharp she tilts
her head at some maladjusted angle . . .

Maimed as a Manx cat. She is
The Arsonist's Daughter. In ninety
eight she learnt to shoot. A talent
for contentious disarray. Her Rhythm
Method is an irreverence of lead . . .

Bette is a trippy laundress,
chews her nails and sorts
figments into story. She has squatted
over a naked flame, sharing her works
like a tragic muse. Hoarse as the Queen
of Hearts from shouting. They open
her up, she's a censored letter . . .

She is so tired that her thought breaks
into a million pointillist scruples.
Her hands become a frieze of needles
and she fails at begging favour . . .

Bette sits sinking into telly's
cool time-zone, spaced out
and slinky; outstaying her welcome.
The wet dream of extra-marital piss
artists, drinker of Bloody Mary's
feudal gauche. Little balking stray,
her *plink plink fizz* starts fires.
A flinching whipcord, rigged to shimmy . . .

The soft rampart of her top
lip gives her away: *this is not
an English girl.* She grows body
hair and eats with her fingers.
Past times in good company, they say,
her suck has more teeth than a B-movie . . .

Bette lives by goosebump and secret
ballot, pins up her hope like skirts,
strutting her eminent silver shoo-wop.
Diana Ross and jellied eels. All good
girly things. Six figure stick-figure,
harkens up the typeset scream
of her own survival: *Take of my body* . . .
Not Christ so much as a True Life
German Cannibal. What is *Christ*,
anyway? A spread-legged compass
for grading curves. Gold digger, she's
stain resistant, a reverse Lady Macbeth!

Bette is a stilt-walking human shield.
Her job is to kid herself and make near
sighted stabs at the written word, study
its swarming congress for premeditations.
She hates you. Her living daylights loom
like on-coming traffic. Her mouth gapes.
Agent of cocky intercept, she gossips
gang-mantra, lurches with leatherfaced
leading men; does full-frontal
nudity, a gospel of knives . . .

Her small smile empties itself
like the kitchen sink. As midnight
moves into prayer position, she is still
awake. In the involuntary hours
the bed becomes a broomstick, and she
is fit for screeching. More diseases
than data can stream. She's not mine,
you know. She's no kin to me. She's not me . . .

Loathing is not flashmob with pillows but a valentine of faint praise.
I could stab you in the mouth, I could. Candles insist on things
like morons. Sacredness is not a serious proposal, stupid stupid
stupid. I'll put a formidable slit in your belly like the skewed seam
of my pencil skirt. Take my picture. I'll strike a pose. Still-life with
insufficient medication . . .

v

Practiced starveling, pressed
into service in my ward
sister's whites. A negligent toughy,
my red hair floats like field-dressing . . .

I have outlived my own
need to be naked. Fingers,
inseparable as orchids
in their perishable potbind . . .

Oh, hands are easily amused.
Their games are simple
and may be copied by children.
Mine were as startled
and important as gloves . . .

My cigarette is strategising.
I wish I was long and lean,
a guitar solo, decanting
sound into sex appeal. But no.
I am a bug-eyed ugly. Poems
are pained and perfect smoke rings.
They tempt fate like tainted meat.
They make me sick to my bad breath
and wishful thinking . . .

Put me on a gurney,
supine and horticultural.
I have a tangent craft, I speak
a caressing acumen. My lips
gather spittle for an alliteration . . .

My open hand is caught
in the conversion of light.
Am I real yet? Can I have
three thousand pounds and my
own cardboard star on the door?
Is there a grant for this? Will you
forward my application for me?

VI

And his voice would clasp me like a crescent moon, front and centre, a confidence trick. Look at how the hawthorn wraps itself up in self-reliant sharpness. I am like that. I fascinate into festive splinters. Men used to come and flip us like frying meat, spread on the mattress in our road-kill coteries: pancaked girlies squashed like foxes. So much for urban renewal, Mother . . .

Poem in which my Grandfather is a unicorn

My drill-bit bonce is a power tool,
pure Black & Decker. I don't joust,
but bore and cork; laborious blue-
collar spirochete. I gauge, I weigh
and counter-sink. Pallid navvy, I
plot courses, grade curves
and warble loony shanties
under a *flimsy,* freeloading moon.

In summer my kinked withers steam
as I doss by the flat, brown pond
and champ at my baccy.
There- with any luck- some stringy,
somnolent blonde will fodder me up
bruised apples; smear Deep Heat
on my sweated flanks.
This is what passes for pleasure.

Winter's worse, and when
that chilly bastard
climbs in at the window
me and my muckers huddle.
In the cold-clammy dark we are a row
of raised middle fingers. We glow, spark
and jar; rare as uranium rods, we are,
and twice as bloody depleted.

Sometimes, the ganger has us gouge
staves in the frozen ground
for *come mister tally man, tally me
a coffin,* marking off The Dead
on The Job. And sometimes
he wants we should lance and spar
and *Toro! Toro!* while the overseers
spill tinnies and lay bets.

It is bad, but not that bad.
Yous can always nuzzle
with some ruddy bawd,
have her hanky-knot
your Billy-beard; there's
the cider-squishy tang of her,
lank and gold as dirty straw.

That, or yous can dream. I dream
of earth what didn't surge or churn
but greened, sweetly, keenly, me
yokeless and shiny, simpleton free.

I dream when we was High Horses,
tilting into groves of gushing sun
to munch at *peerless* pomegranates.

That was long ago, though. Long ago
and far away and maybe only make-believe.
Pretty fiction's well and good, but we
are none of us children. *This* is life, girl,
and in the end I'm glue, you're glue, like the rest.

The Mystic and the Pig Thief

Purple loosestrife: the runaway writes from a traveller encampment.

AUGUST 18, 2003   SMITHY FEN, CAMBRIDGESHIRE.

Dear Pig Thief—

God, these English!
The sun speaks softly to them.
They walk, larded with light,
giving all things permission to grow:
proscenium dogwood, burgundy rose.
Those gardens! Those neat green fingers meting out colour!

I am in love with the English.
They do not love me back.
They love their gardens and children
and the land along the Lockspit path
barbed with stars of cow parsley,
asterisks of damp hemp agrimony,
sour purple loosestrife.
Their love is a possessing.
They do not know the names of things
or how some plants are poison to their horses.

They are afraid of me,
say that I smell
of hot black asphalt,
cigarettes and ferrets.
They are afraid of the dogs as well.
Malkin, mongrel, all of us.

I love them anyway.
It's their gardens that make them afraid.
Their fear is a kind of chivalry.
They want to save the flowers
from cowboy tarmac, work-boots, dog shit.
They've seen how we live.

It is okay.
I am enclosing a knuckle of bud,
an ophry, white with pink around
the rim. This, I think, is my only
theft. Please come soon and see.
It's not like home at all.

Sowing rocks: the runaway writes from a commune in Split of the travellers' eviction from Smithy Fen.

NOVEMBER 11TH, 2004   SPLIT, CROATIA.

Dear Pig Thief—

Behind the house the continents of pine
are becoming tectonic. Soon to shift,
carry us off in a mud slide. Still no word from you.

Did I do something wrong? I worry.
Did your job fall through? Are you back
in The Aquinas Reformatory?

There were three-
hundred and eleven of them,
drove us out of Smithy.

They had meetings.
A woman said that she would like to
blow us all to kingdom come,
then let the pieces stew
in raw sewage.
The papers reported it.
Her son was in Afghanistan.

I don't like it here.
A tense light stretched between the beacon juts.
White regime of water, hammering us flat.
That puberty of cloud! Oh God!
Sky so nude and clean it makes you sick.
We unbutton our blouses and sow rocks,
stripped off and seeding the sea-belly full of flints.

I don't like it here.

Bitter tea with flavoured syrup.
Occipital curve, low winter sun.
That necessary cartilage
of deadwood round the old chalk wall.
Beady, swivel-headed birds, a clutter of wing.
                                        I will come home.
In the morning I lotus my legs.
Dust the iconostasis.
Prise apart the window.
Let the blue chlorinated daylight
sluice the bedroom.
Go over and over your lack of letter.
Someone must have told you
that I am here by now.

Yellow deepening to silence: the runaway replies from Split to a message passed by a friend.

APRIL 23RD, 2005   SPLIT, CROATIA.

Dear Pig Thief—

My seeds have begun reaching!
The poppies, red
as sunburnt Brits abroad,
turn adoringly toward
the light, doing mute hero worship.

My lily's less respectful,
cocks a deaf ear at the din of day,
her yellow deepening to silence.
My lily is a Dietrich, her face a legendary mask.

Mog brought in your message late last night,
and now I'm kneading window boxes, thinking:
don't forget how not to trust. Remember Finn and Breen and
     Colm.
Keep savvy, stay safe. Peel eyes and peep at keyholes. Please.

How was the rally? Your brother?
Bearing his drum in front like a busted gut,
perspiring in the heavy weather. And you?
And your sister? And your brother's wife? And everyone?

Forgive me, I am nervous.
There is fear in this town.
I hang my watching in the window
                         like a lantern.
Don't laugh.
I have my flowers
and my premonitions.
I lit a tealight late last night, for you,
ate fatty pastry with my fingers, went

about with bare feet, wished
I spoke the language.

Souk is a colour you can cry.
I knelt on the floor. It was cold.
A taste like dirty pennies in my mouth.

Pale hypnosis of fire: full of smoke and longing, Pig Thief sends a message to the runaway in Split.

Biddy—

Jonesing you last night. Bones of me up all hours with aching. Does my head in. The bad rheumatics of a wank-attraction, 'cause you pop up in that posh frock out a bowl of blue, like a vision of the Virgin Mary. I miss yous.

That black dress, sleek as a body bag and pushing the tops of your tits together like the domes of skulls. Those English fucks. Who're they? Come home, Biddy. The lads ask after you. There's work to do. How long can you run for anyway? You must know by now how it is, how home is the tin can train that rattles behind you. They hear you / see you / smell you coming. Don't expect anyone else to love you, not out there, not in the real world.

High tonight, like every night. Curfew screwing the silence shut. Like the Bad Old Days. Somebody shot somebody else. Going mad down there. Pale hypnosis of fire on the edge of the cemetery. God knows. But you're in here with me, up in the crow's nest, getting undressed, taking your clothes off in sleepy slow-motion, letting them fall to the floor like the small heaps of ash that you tap from your filter-tip cigarettes. You smell of cheroot and sunrise, Biddy. Titties like the stiff peaks of beaten egg white, elbows stuck out to make folded wings. I could lean forward and touch you, snap your black knicker-elastic and finger the line that it leaves in your skin. Your hair is the colour of Cherry Nyquil. Your lips putting on passive resistance, scratch like prison blankets. Scar on your belly is shining. Inlaid, you are, all pricelessly pearly like a Gibson guitar.

Fuck it Biddy, is it a life where you are? Cadging from gadjo wankers for cash? Pulling your *cross my palm* routine? There's mystic here too: boys bald as Buddha-bothering Krishnas, hanging in cells; towers falling, cups and disks. Hubcaps and robbed copper wire, Biddy. Fuck's sake, you don't have to be afraid. I'm on errands for Jim now. Nobody fucks with Big Jim's boys.

A hemlock of incense: her head done
in by lust and foreboding the runaway
writes as she begins her journey home.

MAY 3RD, 2005   ZAGREB, CROATIA.

Dear Pig Thief—

Home again, home again, jiggity-jig.
Where's that from? I come out
of the rave, melting under K-Y
currents of electric light. I'm so tired
my hands shake like a surgeon
with burnout. But I think I look fine,
streaks of clubland colour in my hair.

       I've been thinking about God. No,
       not that mid-Victorian patriarch
       with his Karl Marx beard. I mean
       the Real Deal. At home, God
       is a granny flat, camp as Carmen
       Miranda, a decked out Drama Queen.

Here, he's more nude, more whole, less
silly. I'm not just buzzing, it's true!
All those angels, beatific bitches, shining
on with repeat prescription pearliness.
I've never felt closer. They remind me
of Mog. They remind me of me.
They remind me of you . . .

Heaven is a Hawksmoor church.
Look, white marble
clarifies the light.
These are the wide,
empty forecourts

in the showrooms of eternity.

Railway stations are holy.
Last night I dreamt that God was only
the spaces between
the words and forms.

This building is classical
but the fine, high ceiling cannot contain my journey.
It makes me think of Hawksmoor
and Heaven.
                    Heaven: that pasteurised Protestant invention,
                        bright as a floodlit garage forecourt.

I am coming.
        Back to the old world, its muck, its gold, it's you.
        Honey-
                drip.
        Cherry-
                pick.
Stretch me between the stanza-pews,
                bend me until the spine of my miscellany cracks.

Heaven is a Hawksmoor church.
Heaven is the wide-winged concrete concourse
of the station at Zagreb.
I empty my emptiness into this.
        Hold me. Breathe me
                like smoke in a bowl . . .

I am moving.
I see birds elocuting winter.
The luminal Bedlam of tangent skyline.
The ghost of a boy, sucking caraway seeds.
An old man. A hemlock of incense.

I'm going to ride
past kitchens lit up
like operating theatres.
Past Jonah stations
full of seadark.

Pig Thief,
keep safe for my coming.
I unravel with the sing of it.
       It travels me, this journey.

Ottoman Tulips, gory black: collected scraps
from a correspondence (unsent). She has
strange premonitions and waxes mystical. He
has visions of her as he thinks of the past.

MAY 7TH, 2005   ON THE JORDAAN, AMSTERDAM.

There is a stillness at my centre,
round and cold as a marble.
I drink dark black priest-piss coffee,
take a fluency of smoke inside myself
until my eyes water . . .

    It is a crisp, expensive daylight
    that crackles like butchers paper.
    Nobody *does* anything.
    City squanders itself –
    a pestilence of flowers . . .

I am the man of La Mancha, my dream is impossible!
It is to be vulgar and supple,
not modestly perverse like fingerless gloves . . .

    My dream is impossible, it talks to me
    in the pandering jibber of birds, or signs
    as pure as a Roman salute; sometimes
    I wear reheated wings and drip like a candle . . .

I am an Icarus. I want
to thrive like flame, lift up my face
to the sun's riffing inquest, become
prophetic and agitant . . .

    It talks to me, muddled
    as rancid butter. I shove
    sullenly at light. I want
    to be frank with arson, a virtuoso scold . . .

I want to slam-dance my flammable ad lib
up, up, up like ninety-nine *Luftballons.*
The crowd are gawping gateposts: who's she,
queen of Sheba? sulking into brilliance . . .

    I must tell you: in my vigil-artillery I lit
    cigs and wicks for the names of The Dead.
    The bedroom glowed with lavish beadwork
    and I, falsely pearled as a courtesan, curtseyed at
        congenial mirrors.

    I thought I saw ghosts there, bowing back at me. Only
        you will understand this . . .

    This is loneliness, you see? Loneliness is work,
    is worked at, is worked up, becomes
    a sanctimonious offering, tries to make
    sadness moral.

    I am the man of La Mancha, my dream is impossible!
    To have you in my hand, like a marble, like a tooth . . .

Biddy—

We gone up Grange and wrecked on rec behind Assumption saw you weeding in the deep trees. Yous were cross-legged, and wise as a crib sheet, sucking the air over your teeth. Someone scattered stars above the prison to gather an intelligence of grief and boredom. Rat-Face said you'd gone to ghost like wild tomatoes gone to seed.

Don't blame you for leaving. Childhood was the habit of hiding, crawling under Daddy's shadow. Don't blame you. But I crave you, like some pregnant woman wanting chocolate, coal and salt. The naked strange of you. Little Drummer Girl, Little Red Fox. The mad damp basket of your copper-coloured hair, broken comb caught like a wrecked ship. You laugh. You are laughing. Your mother despairs.

You tell me one time how a flower is a form of flightless bird. We're cooking potatoes in the open fire. You're too close, flames are making your bangles hot. Soon you'll have a smart on your outreached wrist: *Flower's a form of flightless bird . . .* I'm wondering where you get this stuff.

Maybe I believe you now. Them cypresses, black and hunched as undertakers' mutes. That doomed babble of yellow broom wrapped around the arches is canary, pure canary. Waiting for fire, the lot. And me, equal unable to leave.

I'm looking out over the rec, inhaling the absence of journey, the long green that leads nowhere, the empty space that stands me still. I feel so old. You're in my head, walking the empty canal to Kilbeggan, or weeding in the deep trees, eating seeds with slender fingers.

Pig Thief, wearing red braces,
a second Sebastian, arrowed.
Pulls off his fingers like petals:
loves me, loves me, loves me . . .

He squashes into my brain, beer
can crushed against the forehead . . .

Pig Thief, a tactful croupier,
busies his losing hands. Dispenses
besotted raillery in a woozy stage
whispers: *loves me, loves me, loves me* . . .

Biddy—

I walk the Main Parade in the white hot extremity of afternoon. I close my fist around my feelings. Choke. A canary in a coalmine. I smell petrol and believe in vengeance. My brain's buzzing like when electric things get overheated. Caravans are rocking on their arches, great steel mangers, hot sun slanting off of them. Dogs're dry-humping each other. You're six, Biddy, wearing white gloves, dreaming of fists full of fivers. First summer in The North, learning the language. Fast city. Feast city. Fist city. Beast city. *Harlot and Wolf,* somebody says. City of The Harlot and The Wolf.

The suburbs improvise an afternoon.
I am startled by Turks' Heads,
their colour's bulk:
Ottoman tulips, gory black.
Deep thrombotic knots of scent
and haemorrhagic claret. The stab
of midnight burgundy. A heroism.

I am an Old Wife.
The flowers tell me what to fear.

Pig Thief says *hokum*. He doesn't know
how not to live forever. I dream his head.
It fits the deforming mania of tulips.
Baroque by blunt-force trauma, concave
as a Hapsburg. Smashed in. The Spanish
were cruel.

The colours don't mean what they've always meant.
I thread a recurrent concussion of orange blossom.
It's the tar that feathers me. I am flying to him on an expletive of
green night wings.

Kissing cousins: from an unsent letter (possibly to be treated as a journal entry). Pig Thief writes of his Mystic's return and about his plans for their future.

MAY 16TH, 2005   FLATROCK, NORTHERN IRELAND.

Out of that big, bad hybrid night: she's long in coming and less in sense, my Mystic. Shingle of tears makes her silver. Armour of scales, a moody mermaid Joan of Arc. She's foil-wrapped by the moon and reading the tarot for tourists, dressed in a flourishing skirt, a barbarity of bracelets / Thalers / earrings. Body- pierced prodigal, catching the light. Captive jangle. Jingle jangle. It's an act but she believes it, and she's right too, to find future floating face down in their hands. She showed me once, did mine: livewires cut like hotwired cars, railway pylons spilling sparks, no future in it. She spat for a swimming pool, laughed at me.

From up here you can see the city applying sudden fire like a failed actress putting on lipstick. Ill starred, shabby human ruin, Biddy says. And Biddy's like the city, frail and sprawling, all scrappy flare, and lean, fretting charm. Not for her the pre-recorded wisdom of the gruff and measly blessed, women whose maundering purity of spirit is enough to make you retch. Biddy's no pretender with puffy eyes who tries to micro-manage bliss. My Mystic's not seduced by the *warm fuzzies* of some or other rubbishy abstract noun. Wild hair, clinging and kelping, sweeping the wind at Malin Head, or anywhere. Rare thing. I would marry her.

But she worries me, giving her body to boys, selling it off piece by piece, like wild land sold off plot by plot to greedy fucking developers. It's her loss makes a profession out of losing. Porous as a piece of honeycomb, light and sweet and sickly. Call her honey pie. Call her suntrap. Call her strawberry. She says *so what?* They go through her rich pickings, seagulls on a rubbish tip. It's not the men she's trying to outrun, she says, it's herself. She wants to be weightless, free, full of holes like a sieve for sugar. You get me?

I'd marry her. She paints her toenails and will come to a bad end. Neither of us got the brains we were born with. Should've stayed in the wilds, burnt charcoal and been picturesque, but we crawled out of that dark, incestuous Gaeltacht, slinking and skulking and mangy as foxes. We went to go stew in the tower blocks. Kissing cousins, scrubbers, scallies, scaldies, backwards backwoods chavvy scum. Now we have to make do with each other. Skilled in the pagan practise of clan feud, we take to the night do our various arsons there.

Oh, but she'll come home, combing all catchy-monkey in a maverick spree of Rimmel London, Total Red. Biddy doing poems in the strut of our social housing, voguing in cock-suck counterpoise, bridegroom-broody, loony and *voluptuous*. Her armpits are old fashioned inkwells. Signed and sealed in her Latinate street tags, tatts like a circus strong-man, she's got. Dumb as a ducking stool, they said: *so dense that light bends round her.* They don't know how I covet the slathered starfield of her shoulders. They don't know *shit* from *smart.* Biddy swaggers like a boy in arrogant drag. Expert in sundry jettisons, head butting pigs, kicking shit in.

A mess, and I love her. The whole high-rise is waking, the fluteband boys doing post-ketamine baby steps, or skinning up in skunky stairwells. She's coming home, my Mystic, the gravity grabs at you that way. She says *be careful* but I'm full of the liming fire now. It makes me hard, it ambers me my angel wings. I'm Saint fucking Michael and his fiery sword. I got constellations of shit to sell to make the dark more sparkle. I'm putting diamonds in their eyes. Flatrock is buzzing like a wasp's nest tonight. We're going to make our money. I'm going to marry her.

The orrisroot: his Mystic arrives home. Unable to find him she pushes a note under the door.

There have been burnings. Too many places
have the narrow privilege of shrines.
There is police tape: guy ropes for holding
All Souls to the ground.

I am a stranger here.
You are not in your ziggurat.
You are nocturnal now,
a night-breather,
a poisonous plant.
You go about in silver
Subarus, vibrating to bass.

Who planted the orrisroot
and slowed time to a crawl?
It has all the selective deafness
of a white tequila worm.

I stand in the porch light
counting up satellite dishes:
the dread black pox
of some tropical disease.
I see Flatrock has become virulent.

Where are you?
Dislocated somewhere
like a floating fucking rib.
Was it you who planted the orrisroot?
Made the window boxes stink of cats and gin.

We were hungry: Mystic writes to the Pig Thief's brother, on the morning of his funeral.

JUNE 1ST, 2005   FLATROCK.

Frankie—

I don't know what to say.
Inflating the blank page
behind me like a parachute,
I stutter and gurn and bite
my lip.

Some people have regular
Swiss Army Mouths, a word
for every occasion. I've got
a dank fury that taps the bone.

I wake up in the night with a thumb-
sucking thirst. His death is something
scraped across the brain, a knife
on burnt, black toast.

The sky is dark as vatted wine,
and you are going to torch the van
today. I will turn my Claddagh
ring outwards. It's what we do,
follow the few breadcrumb
remnants of dumb tradition,
any tradition. We have our
common place Catholicisms,
the boys with macho
wassail, our *ad hoc* sad *pomana.*

He wouldn't want this. I remember
going out dancing, punked up
to Psycho-Ceilídh, Pig Thief mishearing
Van Diemen's as Bad Demons, like Hell

was empty and all the devils had rocked
up here in their marlin spikes and thug
life swank. You couldn't teach him anything.

I know you are angry. I came too late.
But don't keep me away. I am suffering too.
Nobody else will ever
        pour their poetry
                into my ear
                        like petrol through a letterbox.

This loss grinds momentum out. And fire.
Give me permission to stay and to become dutiful,
dance my dunce's attendance on his ghost.

Don't be angry because I knew him
better than you, knew that intermittent
fizz inside, a strip light / a strip search /
a search light / a nakedness that became
its own captivity after not very long.

We wanted –

No, I don't know what we wanted.
I just know how to be hungry.
We were hungry.

Frankie, don't blame me.
Don't hate me. I tried to tell him.
All I can be now is here. Let *home*
close over my head like water.

Feral Children: a reply from the Pig Thief's brother. He tells her not to stay.

JUNE 2ND, 2006   FLATROCK.

Little Sister—

Mother called you *road apple*. It was a prophesy,
of sorts. You have to understand, there is no home.
For you there is only the body.

Get up.
Put on your black jeans
and your green silk camisole top.
Put on your boots
and your fingerless gloves.
Put on your khaki coloured
Parka, talisman made
from whale bone.

You used to hide out in the kennels.
You used to do portents for storms.
You used to solemnise animal pacts,
pacts with foxes, horses, crows.

One time I caught the pair of yous,
grunting and rubbing your bloods
together. I caught you doing twin
talk, the mad telepathic pidgin
of all feral children. I never liked
how you wore wildness as a private joke.

Get up. Let the ouija
of your precious West Wind
spin you far. You are full
of cryptic momentum,
self-contained as a bullet.

He's in you. In the packed
powder of you, seeking spark.
It was always going to happen this way.
I don't want to watch.
      Gather your tarot and go.

The reproachful carnality of orchids or lilies:
Mystic leaves a letter in the ashes of the van.

Pig Thief—

I mustn't scratch things in soot.
I wasn't here. This is merely the mind
in its trivial cinders, thrown on a fire.

This poem wants magic to be real,
wants all my conjurations
to connive a boy, a prancing tenant
in a tight black tee.
And you would be sheeny and real again,
no longer griping in the earth.

The squanderous grace of an alley cat, you!
It gives me pangs, it does, to do without
your flattened shadow, concertinaed in
between the bed and the bedroom wall.

But I have to be hard. Hard as a diamond drill-bit.
I can't put on your Celtic shirt, inhabit
its emptiness; cry by the cross, clinical light
of a mute television. I have been *given my cards.*
They show disks and towers and blue-green serpents, rampant.

You're too good for grieving anyway,
like a fancy frock too posh to wear.
I'll make a deal with you. The Dead
are always making deals:

when I think of you it won't
be flowers, the reproachful
carnality of orchids or lilies.

You will be dogshape
and bogwraith. You will
be sliver and friction,
and under the igloo light
of an orifice moon, go
crooning and keening.

When I think of you it will
not be dust, the hostile greed
of empty rooms.

I will seek you
in the deviated optic light
of bar snugs,
in the arterialising gush
of service station coffee,
the whole round wounded world.

I will put on my boots.
I will see you on the ceiling,
galvanized by *rough magic* and *tough luck.*

I will go outside, breathe in.
Smell of cum from the lindens.
      Sky. Tree. River.
These things frame the unconditional.

Nothing grows here but the weather: Mystic writes from the road, fragments from a journal of her journey.

Pig Thief—

A haunting is really a slow seduction.
I am an apt pupil. Somebody's paying
the sea out like silk,
                        your guerrilla
                                necromancy with it.
I am taking the coast road. You goad
my moaning North to storm. I stagger
on the sealegs of my loss, hear you
singing. Bickering ricochet hardwire
handsome, you! You're gone and my
head hurts so hard the loud light creaks.

I should get drunk and see angels,
but I don't trust myself. Someone
once said that that our generation
would be born *with bricks in their fists.*
You have joined the rigid and ignorant
dead, men like milk cartons, opened
up by the edges of their wounds.
You ask me am I *feart?*

I'm not afraid of farmers
or chemical spray or dogs
or *Trespassers Will Be Shot!*
or barbed wire or lorries
or lorry drivers or social
workers or policemen
or motorways.

I skip along in frequencies, my all-
black bandwidth crackles. The cold
is pithing my lips.

I am walking out the coast road,
nothing grows here but the weather.
The smoke is swelling the sky.
Burn back the corn. Raise a stink,
the scorched and soggy earth, a prayer.
I am not scared.

Pig Thief—

The sky. The sea.
Boundless and soapy. Guilty.
Not one wilderness, but two.

We pulled the leaves from the branches.
We sucked the meat from the bone.
The sun like a sniper's bead is training
small and cold and close across the fields.

This country has a habit of disowning you.
Even the stories of local children leave
this place for dead. It is full of vigilant
emptiness. The light inhabits the upper
rooms like a jealous spinster.
I will stay here.

Jehovah sequoia stand poised to offer
me a blessing. Goosebumped recluse
among the madding of the winds.

My Pig Thief—

I dreamt it again:
fire inflating the van.
In my dreams you are inside,
My Viking Pig Thief! A tarred
squire with a golden sword . . .

I count the days
like a child racing rain-
                  drops.

I've had enough of love,
it saps the will like a Sunday
morning hangover. I am full
of the same illegible bellyache
as always.

Nothing changes. I won't
give you up. They should've
burnt me. Stupid to think
you were tied to *stuff*,
that *things* could let you go.

Anyway, you'd not been back
for months. Should've burnt me,
burnt everything. What if fire
doesn't want to set you free?

In my dream, your open hand,
a monkey's paw, holding
nothing but its three wishes . . .

I count the days,
leaking *lust* and *hurt*
like a cracked thermos.

In time, they tell me, I'll learn
a deprogrammed plainchant, and not
spit grief like teeth. They tell me
that the heart's not a smashed up
watch, but it is.

And what if fire's for binding to,
for knitting up the living and the dead?

I dreamt it again, the fire,
you and I are fused
the way that broken bones mend.

I couldn't beg more light, only breathe.
Only draw a precaution of darkness around myself.
Pry the night like a peeping Tom. Make a shy
conspiracy of my respirations. Put one
indifferent, serviceable leg in front of the other.

On the hill behind the compound, six
sturdy, plaintive men are tending
to small heaps of fire. Little
ulcerating lights, they twinkle
and blister. Not a colour but a pain,
a twinge in the pink of the gum.

I slide along a ridge of sly,
greenblack pine. I slide
into our dense ancestry of trees.

Men jab with sticks.
They goad and coax.
They flog the fire
to a spittle of crude exhaustion,
to throttles of hot ash. I divine
this shit, I am a spooky wife!

This night, more sincere and more guilty
than any other night, up to its elbows
in excavation, lording it out of the lean earth.
A hollow bombast like an Ibsen husband.
I hate this night. I am leaving.

I am leaving the country, this failed Bethlehem.
I am leaving its raw carbohydrate mass, its defunct nativities.
Birth is ugly here, a baby is a glottal stop.

Rumours spread like foot and mouth.
The farmers, sorry Herods, all sing sweet
Leonard Cohen laments to a culling.
I will be no farmer's wife! I will be no child bride! I will not wait
for the purifying Light of the Lord to selectively deafen me. No
    more of this.

Silos like sacked empire, old
and wearing slowness as a wisdom.
No more arable lethargy, the docile regimen
of a maternity ward. No more puppies or kittens
or kiddies or chickens or piglets. No more selfish
superabundance. I will be no Solomon to do the divvying
work. I will pull up no roots. I will pluck no feathers. I will
carry no children.

The country is crouching, gathering its creeds, winding
up the red thread of its long memory. But I am leaving.
They throw up fences as I go, fishbones catching in a windpipe.
There are houses now. And houses, like all scavengers, hunt in
    packs.
I outwit the wires and Volvo-jaws of these. I outfox them all,
those Barratt Home hyenas. I am leaving. Longing is better
than slow corrosion. A hunger that chases its tail, that chews on
    itself.

Echo-locating: Mystic scrawls a disjointed message to Pig Thief's brother.

JANUARY 22ND, 2006   IRELAND.

~~The junction lit up~~
~~in lewd bordello sodium.~~
~~The horizon line is a rotten filament,~~
~~eaten through in places. I have not missed~~
~~the din of cities. Noxious realism. The church~~
~~on the flyover, its Paramount Pictures corona of stars . . .~~

Frankie—

This is just to let you know,
you needn't write back. I'm dropping
stones in the water, is all.
I'm scattering breadcrumb proofs.

It's okay, really. I go through the night
like a cigarette through silk. I sing
to keep myself company.

I am picking the distance clean.
Nana saw me all right for money,
and later there's always busking.
I can do fortunes again if I get
as far as Brighton.

You won't worry.
I don't think of it too much.
Only, it's hard to remember
which one of us is dead.

Love to the family
and to the dogs and to the whole skanky
cornucopia of Flatrock after closing time.

Locating an echo,
              Biddy.

Slender in sway: mostly undated excerpts from Mystic's journal, written from London, England.

Pig Thief—

Their methods are many
for not being you.

It rains, mostly. I sit in cafés
watching women. Women in
cardigans and crash diets, pulling
hairs from their sleeves. They are
the same as me: a cheek chewing drab
with a social conscience, plucking
out eyebrow hairs like arrows.

Or I watch men,
coughing up phlegm.
Their mouths are the piss
darkened doorways
of council houses.

Their love is promiscuous with bruises,
more breaks in
than a mermaid's tattooed tail has scales.

I name each intake of breath: *diddums,
honeybunch, angelcake, soldier.* It's so
cold. Sundays are slow death by Nestlé,
autumn defrauding the trees. I picture
you banging the frost off your socks.

Pig Thief—

These lips are soft, colourless suckers, blooming like mushrooms.
I am taking deep, frilly breaths and trying to calm down. In the
bedroom the icons, Baby Jesus and assorted saints are trapped in
their lightbulb moments, frowning. Their heads are tempting Ferris
wheels. Mary's tits are missionary lilies, quaint refineries of curds
and whey; milk, honey and draught bitter. Her glad eye is angled
off-stage. Popes are blinged-up pimps, they shuffle their ruby
slippers in the wings.

Also, there are photographs, uncles stuffed with useful rural
fortitude, and all their pale, best-bemoaned wives, crouched like
flying monkeys, stirring a pot with a stick. In my head there is child
abuse and cabin pressure. My ancestors travelate at tangents, sliding
by, dependable and kettlebellied, beery, dirty. They do expeditious
vagrancies, bringing loose tea and white goods, the Homage of the
Magi.

And now my veins are an antfarm, and now the spectres, in their
headless revenue, come blizzarding out of the walls, and now the
mirror carves me like a pumpkin, suave mimic whose smile is
vegetable matter. Why does she grin so? A child roused by a bell,
I lift up my arm and the toyed-with wrist unravels its pennants and
heraldry. I decipher the seductions of The Dead, my edible breasts
are elaborate truffles, my name is Agatha, Lamb of God, white as a
sanitary napkin.

I am dropping down where all is dust, where all the dust is:
dusty catshit shabtis, wrapped in chalky shrouds, dust in the lines
around a smoker's mouth, dust in dog hair and asbestos, dust
that clogs the CPU; that closes the throat, that makes the eyes red.

I am naked, all shiny pistes, vertical and stern. My belly is a glitzy
plaza, my pubic hair makes prim laurels around civic-minded

shrines. There is a machine shop crashing in my head, crashing like cash registers, like unmanned aircraft pile-driving into buildings. I am leaving. The icons in aphid clusters, the nuns folding themselves up, weighty tomes, experimental birds.

Pig Thief—

Night lights me up like a fruit machine. I stoke the streets with my next-to-nakedness. Shoulder shows black bra strap and tatt, the lily, the phoenix, the plough and the stars. I bite my lip, I keep my teeth closed. They don't know me. They can't read. Your Mammy called me *road apple:* windfall of white flesh apple core curves, sexy as a scimitar. Think of me as sweet Eve Pudding. I dance down the cracks out of King's Cross / Grey's / The Rat / Costcutter / The Station / The Terminus. White heads roll, a mortar of blossom. Girls in the bloom of our crash and burn. Incendiary oleander, slender in sway. They can't read. A collapsed vein is not fig vine snaking a silver birch. Pale's not for pure. Bone's not for wishing. I'm not Julia Roberts or Lizzie fucking Siddal. Freshmen, red eyed and dishevelled, declaiming the flood in the shitfaced pick of their verbose virginity; builders with B. Techs, wiping their hands in my hair. I'll tell you all a secret:

Men are fucking idiots. They see a sob run the length of my arm like the recoil from a gun. They see the promiscuous pinks of my eyes, the lurid weepers of widows. Say *weak.* They cotton on the lowercase curl of my spine, my cufflink ankles, my crummy morsel nakedness. They see how I tremble my gasleak mirage, I shake. Say *weak.* They see me and sex me my nuptial bud, split, the grooved hoof of an iris. They see the spooling of slow whorehair, yellow-blonde red-blonde bottle-blonde, tabby. Small pulse like the drip of a leaky tap. Say *weak.* I get to keep them company the way fruit keeps maggots. This flesh-confessional does my head in. They don't know me. It's not for lack of love that I'm falling through cities like snow.

Pig Thief—

I sing you. I sing all the long limbed lead lifting district boys, codding the sky-miles white as lime for Theft and Grace. My belly still aches from the feast day of your dirty cutlet nakedness, my tits weighed in the white flames of your handspan, snag of your lip-ring ripped on my dog-tooth; your pubic scrum, not black, but twizzles of dark, green, fried sea cabbage. I sing you.

I sing you, passionate criminal. I sing the carny cult of your infidelity, your lovely hypocrisy, all of the straight-world girls you went down on in waltzers and ghost trains. I sing how you juddered me like a Ford Cortina with shot suspension, on a mattress, in a caravan, at three A.M.

I sing the long limbed district boys, their inquisition's discipline. Skangers in sovvies and trackies, trekking the Soviet supergrass dawns between curfews. I sing the boys out of Ógra, those Omagh boys who won't live to know better. I sing their lips, wet with poitín and petrol, with midnight oil and a blasphemy of coffee dark as bull's blood. I will chant their masochist's catechism long into slender neck of the night and leech light from a moon like a puncture wound. This, the Goth Rock nonsense of my grieving.

Love, I am crying my great big blue Billie Holiday heart out. My love, font of all ignorance, my people, my home. I sing for you. For Frankie, in all his apolitical poverty. For Grandfather, his dutiful, inscrutable poverty. Nana, her small-boned, back-bent poverty. Aunts, doubled up like stab victims in the narrow groins of churches for the pious, the pitiless, the fascism of poverty. Cousins, into gang violence and football, dog fights and football, rap music and football, endless fucking football, a purgatorium of football. I sing you.

Oblivious prodigal, gone into the dark to make it yours, sleep it like a subway, cider-piss its walls and sing for a percussion of cash. I metabolise this music.

> Cry me a river and God will deliver me
> Sallying forth in his pallid white livery
> Taking my hand while the sun is resounding,
> Morning is breaking and grace is abounding . . .

Pig Thief—

This is the future: the Thames as silver as all celluloid, me, moving down a discarded ribbon of light, sifting the hot topsoil of the night with the sneaky tenderness of scavenging vermin. This is the future: the river a bolt of shot silk. The docklands are dissolving. London, packing herself away. I attempt a prediction, fail at even this.

Through Deptford. I dream of chickens, a conspiracy of white feathers. Deptford's got shit to put holes in your hardware, they said. They said go, be a beautiful junkie, fragile as a figure of speech in the grim and sleepy disciplines of morning, be a vajazzled siren with machine-tooled sundry charms. All the cool kids are doing it. Fauxhemian Rhapsody! Disreputable and frail, resourceful and with gaps between your teeth, made up with the wobbly fineness of a pantomime dame, they said. Oh, I'll be special and I'll be rare.

And I bead along a line of light. Qatari Towers are knife crime. Richter spikes for scaling metric death. Because *this* is the future, and I'm lost in a million chemical conjurations. This city tastes of refrigerated light. London gets under my skin in fat kernels of malarial sickness. This honey coloured parasite traverses the blood. I shudder out of oesophageal darkness, dreaming of skittish white horses. I want to leap like scalding fat from the overground concourse. I want to find a pure deep dark like a hole,

[85]

no phosphorous cosh, no libidinous electric. I want an unstupefied moon, saintly in its shining. My perfumed wrist smells like a sickroom. Me and some man who looks like you, welded together in mutual faceache.

When you feel the fire of the Holy Ghost
Go through you like a dose of salts
There's nothing left to offer but lament;

When the fisher of men's mortal souls
Comes to rake you o'er the coals
All that you can do boys is repent . . .

Pig Thief—

My heart is something soft, green and tender, a pithed peyote bud. I must cover myself in silence like a seed in soil. I went to confession, offered up my small, circular, self-defeating sins ~~and~~
and nothing. Disappointment and relief are the closest of conditions.

Did you know, an exorcist does not draw a demon like brown into a needle? It is about making you hollow, so they can pack you out with God and light, the bowl of a briar pipe stuffed with tobacco. I used to breathe smoke on the mirrors. We used to breathe smoke on the mirrors.

The birds walk with their wings behind them, the crossed fingers of superstitious lovers. The words have put on furs and gone out hunting. I think I'm going away. I make music but it isn't enough. They lay hands on me, playing at faith healers. I've forgotten how to read. It's cold. Winter's wedlock whitens things: carparks, pitbulls, binbags, breath, whores. I try to give gifts of my fists. They are oysters. Hard and tight. I am an oyster. Hard and tight. Making a bloodsport of my dressmakers' scissors. Sky is a blue vacuity of long standing. Assume a celibate circle. Have more sense than to cry.

[86]

I can live my life under English skies
Where comforts all are cold
But I'm still a slave to an early grave
At the end of a winding road . . .

Pig Thief—

Can't think. Brain is crammed with night and booky dust, like a library on a bank holiday. With less defiance than music I will walk out into this long inelastic night, under the white hot suppurations of stars, lanced above the bulbous two-backed beast of London, England. A synaptic fucking of the True North, this. The words are unspeaking themselves. My body dissolves   in   to   d i s t a n c e s.

Islington, the greedy graves are eating the flowers. I haul myself through the raised hackles of the morning, cackling, addled, a Weird Sister in wraparound glasses. I smoke this hag-riddance for a spell of protection. Man calls me *Whore! Gypsy scum! Cum-dumpster!* Calls me *Hole!* and uses me like a landfill. I crawl. On aching knees feeling empty as a spent shell-casing. Or else I'm pacing, jonesing on the very last legs of my lonesome. I can't get free. Spat on, knocked bandy, or fattened in a hospital, the morality of starving. Therapy. Share-alike with dumbfuck twelve-steppers. Refugee refusenik natter in rooms that smell of wet dog and school dinners. Some choice. Anyway, I'm not sharing you. Or Flatrock, ever.

Flatrock being the cold, hard business end of an occupation packed into us. The fear. Not of what happened but what it meant. Boys in backs of vans. Men in ugly, empty houses. Nearside slabs of fathers, drooling brew. I had to go. But I tread a circle.

Can't think. Your lips. My lips. A gentle pressure. A left foot pressing a break pedal. Your finger. My hollow. The dry creek bed of my cheekbone. It is not enough to say *arid* or *empty*. Lot's wife is landscape, particulate, granular. My lips. Spit forms like the bubbles on a pan of boiling peas. All flowers come to powder in the end.

The woman at The Death Laundrette: from a madhouse in England, Mystic writes her reflections.

DECEMBER, 2006   SAINT JOHN OF GOD'S, LONDON.

Pig Thief—

I hold music like a spoon holds an egg.
Light dilates to cover the ground, my hands,
my legs, my spinning centre. I will keep
anniversaries. I will carry on.

Some things shouldn't be spoken of. This is not
the presence of a ghost like the pressure of a hand.
You have become a starlit geography. You are
          the city, the body, the river, the bedrock.

A haunting is death repeating itself.
This is The Death Laundrette. Women's
Work, sifting the soiled griefs like small
clothes. Be well, we are told. I will be well.

I have put on fennel and columbines: mostly
undated excerpts from Mystic's working
journal, written from London, where she
has decided to study. She meets a man
there. She meets several men there.

Dear Pig Thief—

They do not flinch when I speak. Forgetting doesn't happen, it is
something that you do. It is a form of erudition. I study them. They
are like Latin phrases, they can be learnt, if not exactly understood. I
am reading a great deal. Poets, mostly. They infuriate me.

Nana knew the truth of April's so-called *cruelty*, how the shells
fell, disseminating the doctrine of each squat logic. A delinquency
of light played over the Old Familiar Places, and a degenerate star
scattered its incoherence far and wide. There is no *good* or *bad*.
There are no sides, just patented atrocities. World War Germans
doing genocide. And the English, shooting or starving or beating a
little kid's brains out in a stairwell. History isn't something that just
happens to us. Yeah, maybe no one is good.

I think about Nana. Nana after Easter, the silence long and narrow
as a railway carriage; her brothers gathering rags and sticks while
she made tea for men and talked of wincing matters. Maybe no one
is good. Habit becomes ritual by dint of tired absorption. Those
carping Carpal Tunnel kids, handing it down, passing it on. And
this is currency. This is custom, this hate, this killing. We see
ourselves depicted as goblins or zombies, stage-dive Irish, boozy
Boucicault bogie men. The nightly news has a name for them, for us.
This is normal. This is simply What We Do. You and Big Jim's boys
picking up where those other Doctor Frankensteins left off. Makers
of monsters / monsters. No, I know now, nobody is good.

April was always the bronzing month, pollinating God from polished surfaces, from out of the potholes, the bullet holes, the holes left in buildings. April makes speeches. April invites you to touch the clammy brick of the surrender house. That angsty damp is History. April has built a Hilton next to the prison.

April will speak more light, from the strictness of its showers the books will come with spread wings against the cormorant sky. *I* will write. A cleanliness of page awaits me, expressionless and tidy as a bed in a Dutch hotel. This is the reality of *rising*. It is not The Dead. It is sea mist, beginning its long cringe inland, washing our feet with its hair. Yes, I have words for April also. Gridlocked grimy not belonging song, our land our home our nightmare too, for all our distance.

Come June you will be a small, red circle like an insect bite. No one is good. How long will it take before you are dust, a soft flourishing falling into drifts with the persistent politesse of static?

> Mary, please have mercy
> These things you must forgive;
> A man must have forgiveness,
> Or how is he to live?

Pig Thief—

These flat skies scheme rain. The narrow magnolia doorway frames a strategy of limbs; white hygienic shoulder-blades curve like a horse's jawbone. The glass concocts a narrow plank of back, a rind of wrist reflecting in the cabinet's cool steel. A redundancy of hip joint cuttles into focus.

Dark denim jeans slant across the floor. Your body rises from your clothes like steam. The water is a fast astringency of heat. It is eight fifteen. Oh come, spook me to my crooked centre. I have put on fennel and columbines. I am waiting in the bathtub for your witching.

My fingers cling your lips like lichens. The tiles will squeak their own night sweats. The bathroom condescends to dream. A monitor is blipping in my head. I masturbate with green fingered care. *This* is magic.

No. No good. Cabinet / mirror / shower-stall / sky / and you. These flat surfaces find me out. These flat surfaces flatten me.

But I would be a grig wheel, yawing wicker, eel-dense, full of teeming fit to bursting fins and tails. Open window. Let in sky. Conspire to rain. Remember where you are. The dark will stink of cold. I hanker for creeping, devious water. Not for sticking plasters / Pantene / Bio-Oil / my own hospitable nakedness. Wipe glass with hand. Fold photograph. Pick up clothes.

Pig Thief—

It was you, running
through our fingers,
a rope trick, left our
wrists to hang
like lucky rabbits' feet,
all connection severed
between the brain
and its bruised fruit.

I was *so shocked.* I went
into the kitchen, opened
the cupboards, put on
my coat, took it off
again, looked behind
the sofa for pound coins.
I forgot to take the kettle
from its Hopi spiral.
I scalded its flat, brass palm.

The paper folded you into
your proper paragraphs:
age and height and skin tone,
school career and *fealty.*
These words scoot
across the tongue, a dog
with the shits, dragging its arse.

England, slap-happy
with rude awakenings,
never hurt so hard.
The pain of it, I swear,

it kills your sense of taste.
I'm numb as forty fags a day.

It was you, and now
I test my hate with my teeth,
a prospector biting a counterfeit coin.

There are things I cannot tell you. I am ashamed. I have gone to be English in an A line skirt, and to practise erotic austerities. The first of these is a folding in of fire: incanting on the carpet in front of daytime television, brushing blueblack hair to the point of near combustion, waiting for the telephone to ring. The next is conjugating empathy in lieu of a French verb, acquiring a bedside manner like a private nurse. The third is *scrubbing up* to become appropriately packaged, a mean recidivist vixen in a green silk shirt . . .

I do not like this version of myself, but even less I like the underwhelming menace of *home*, little town of kickbacks and fiddles, where women are squirreling victims who hide money under floorboards. Pig Thief, I hate my own mildewed come-hitherness, a bloody repurposed trollop with violet dumplings for tits. But it's all I know, this buzzkill kerfuffle of bodies, or worse, a faux refrain-sterility. Neither pose becomes me much . . .

In Moscow I went to Lenin's tomb. I saw him laid out: a dud dead red Snow White! Such a self congratulating carcass, put away under a Perspex dome. Formaldehyded slap-head, looking for all the world like a fibreglass folly in a fishtank. And I stood there having a priori apologies for thought. My feet hurt and I envied him. I envied him his lilies and his very waxy deadness, a bonkers cross-eyed prom queen, besieged by oily flowers. I got you a postcard. I had such radical ideas, and my earlobes were see through like lettuce. Those were the days! Hanging out with the gender specific dead, looking for bits of the world to bring back. I felt well free. I fancied myself a- I fancied myself . . .

There are things I cannot tell you. I have a *date,* sucking on a lozenge as I go to meet a man who buys me thigh-high patent leather boots and likes long words for being sad. I drink a *lot* of coffee. The espresso machine fans its dirt migraine back at the blood. I hate how he says *expresso,* slack mouth mauling the hungry hot *pronto!* of the word. My body needs coffee in order to function. My body is a tragic capacitor, sucking down thoracic smack. I like how it beats my heart. Men don't beat my heart like that. My lovers are a series of poxy culprits, slack session men, an adequate remix of fetching faces, sampled into purist groove. They talk too much, becalmed on tranqued out plateau, fourth floor, beige, South Bank . . .

I get vertigo here, London's all on levels. Vauxhall, apoplectically Caucasian, slurring its body heat. When I go to meet men I take the stairs. I hope I'll slip and break my neck. The scrapedback blonde of a low winter sun, the sky severe as a Croydon facelift. Bonnington squat party, and lentils like love beads, so hard you'll break your fucking teeth. Friends keep setting me up. Nonplussed corpuscles shunt me south of the river and back. I am a stonewalling ghost of a girl, I toss in a straighbacked chair like a light sleeper. I amass a deficient vocabulary of paper cups and lack grace. Friday nights find me fudging a kiss that is mostly gums, mishap zigzag heap of teeth. They expect the poor to be streetwise. Our fucking is merely a tendency of fingers. Nice boys, they are, whose Heimlich grasping dislodges a rib . . .

Oh Pig Thief, I want to thrust my elbow into his diaphragm with the violence of a poltergeist. How dare he not be you?! I plant my legs apart, the red pillars of a Shinto temple: *come annava go if you think your 'ard enough.* Sex is heavy self-effacement, nothing more. I want to stand on the street corner, bellow Word of God like a ticket tout. I'd like to be mad. My shrill voice echoing the siren's desire to lose itself. I want to outrun my voice like an ambulance. Or drink its equivalent: coffee, coffee, coffee, till the small heart stops . . .

Little girls improvise mourning songs: 'Dear
John' letters. Mystic cannot be happy with the
men she meets. They do not understand her.

J—

You seem to think that History
could mop up pain, the way
white bread mops up brown sauce.

And you say *don't exaggerate,*
as if such loss was not
the stretching out of feeling
on a hot wash.

And Pig Thief dropped,
a dead-headed rose. I snapped
like the tooth of a tortoiseshell comb.
Pure folksong, darling, incidental . . .

J—

This is a starlit grudge match.
I tremble
like an imperfectly set hairdo.

We stand there, working ourselves up
into complicit rages. Oh, don't let's
be reasonable about this. Let's throw
shit at each other. I'm serious. I am
sincere as a skin-complaint.

~~I haven't been happy since~~
I haven't been happy . . . .

J—

London's brimming snowwhirl
all around me. Your right eye
is moving, a swivelling planchette.

I am not plump or social, my mouth's
no horny portal. A lowfalutin *femme
enfant*, you never really loved me . . .

J—

You carve your meat like a bad Sangoma.
There are too many wounds on your plate,
my dear.

While you were being forcibly improved by the Eng
Lit Department at your school, I was spelling Rimbaud
Rambo (as in *First Blood*, 1982). This is what is known
as Cultural Disjunction . . .

The white wine, under its own
crisp centrifuge, flattens us both
to the backs of our chairs. I'm a
spread-eagled ankh in my black dress.
You think about sex. You grab your greedy
garlic breaths from spaces in between us.

I watch the sunlight, acute
on your fork, and think of him
in sovvies, a rare Christmas of fingers!

J—

Bent double in fervent bulimia, my wet
pigtails are sigils on my damp neck. I do
my own brand of horse-faced delirium.
I see you clock the high maintenance manga
of my *baby blues* and shake your head.
True grit formalist, you despise me, refuse
to commit professional suicide. You have
a wife. Oh, bully for you!

J—

I hate hearing myself described
as damaged, like a shop soiled skirt
with a split zip . . .

I've told you before, how that year
is a Black Mathematical Hole, but you
go on, picking the bones out of fish,
discussing the Print Medium. *Print
is dead,* you said and smirked . . .

I'm coming apart
in rag trade ruins
You don't look up.
A fly lands on your arm.
My ignorance
is a form of protest.
You will not understand this . . .

You will go on eating. Your world
has condoms and allotments, magazine
subscriptions, bottled water, gym membership;
a modicum of dictionary lust, weekend
breaks and Neighbourhood Watch.

My tradition is not a technicality.
Little girls improvise mourning songs
as part of their education . . .

K—

To whisper like polite informants
when the sky is *ice and a slice,*
and this precocious Toytown folds
in its agreeable feudal bunkum.

This is our mission, you will
light a fire. I'll see how
a blurred flame fancies itself.
Nice, to be warmed
by a twee heat. Looking down
at the lawns, they are putrid with dew . . .

Now, tie me to a chair
to stop me scuffling seaward.
This is your mission, I'll play
my part, answer all
your questions
with the correct degree
of requisite malice.

I'll skivvy kisses too, bite
on you like a leather strap.
Forlorn and gormless man!
Watch yourself, you might like it!

My mob are gone. *Foreign
Johnnies* with big ideas.
I'm left here, this hospice
of bridges. I'm left to you,
a shameless Ichabod among
the other gallivanting quacks.

These mountebanks, dressed
for Doctor Strange. I hate
them, and howl
for the howling coast . . .

Tie me up, then. I long
for a light that brindles
like a living thing. Nothing
lives here, only the ramrod
regressions of term time;
these fly-specked nights
when you are a weedy kid
with a reedy voice, blotto
on weak grog and *no match*
for the *red flag* of my fists.

Perhaps we *deserve each other*.
During the day I skive around,
write obscenities in chalk
any chance I get . . .

I cherish you childishly, *a Big
Wuss*. And me, I'm full of a special
hate. Not contempt. Not quite. Not yet.

When the world ends: mostly undated excerpts from Mystic's journal, for the year 2008.

Pig Thief—

The English have their hysterias too.
Bombs on buses. Bombs on trains.
Are we any more selfish
because our disasters are local?

It isn't love I cannot feel, but sympathy.
There is no mercy in me. I am
pitiless and sentimental: Norma Desmond
in a necklace of Thalers. We are forced
to the long look of things. It makes us
parochial, shrewd and cold . . .

Maybe we shouldn't have *swarmed* into the cities. But our people
come in from that green, irreligious space beyond. They pushed their
way into Flatrock like weeds cracking the concrete. And we spoiled
it for them, for the others, their idea of themselves, their Struggle,
their God. Our image of eternity was not the same as theirs, it
ran in both directions. Picture a past like a sea without tides. An
endless reflection of emptied-out sky. Not heroic at all, but stoic,
you see? No religion but the weather, no myth but survival. The
crude momentum of retribution to roll us all downhill. A gob full of
gathered moss, pseudo-crusties speaking greenness slantly . . .

Does Father God have mercy
On a sinner such as I?
A man must have forgiveness
Or how is he to die?

Pig Thief—

And the sun come up over the camp, a lump
rising in the throat.
The brook was cooking its small fish.
We pressed our feet to the cold-holding stones
like your grandmother fervently kissing her rosary.
It was Sunday.
You climbed on the waste-pipe. We heard dirty water
like Chinese whispers
tell secrets to the depth of its python dark. It was holy.

                              Suddenly a bird! An Icarus!
Your lips open, a stone
split apart by the heat.
Take my hand and *run!*
to The Wasting Space.

Green places got their own gravity.
It's this that I miss the most.
Trees filter time as well as light. We'd make our slow
                    descent into the half-past five
                              like deep-sea divers,
                                        sinking.
I remember drinking the smell of it. Fox-
freighted, piss-
pungent, illicit like a cinema.
A scrum of stunted pines
behind the rec ground,
a reminder that once we'd been wild:

far as the tarmaced car-park.
Far as the concrete overpass.
Far as the prison
       and the road pointing *South*.

You come to me, Pig Thief.
Your hands flashed small
       and white
       and brazen
against the navy of my blazer.
Dowry of *shit-fucks!*
heaping the air between us.

              This is The Wasting Space. We will tell stories.

The sudden shelter of the trees
leaves a ringing in our ears,
an echo like the hollow crash of surf.

I slit your hand like the skin of an apple.
I slit your hand like the belly of a fish.
Mix with me, Pig Thief,
my blood's not bad but it's hungry.
It's drinking the hole in your hand.

Sometimes there's an autumn
of hairless women. Pages of porn
torn into shreds
of shiny thigh / grinning, goofy, custard-
pie / cum-shot faces / lips big
with blow-job collagen.

Plug up the holes in the ground / staunch
Nature / insect myriads / birds
mend the spiky
mess of their nests
with the loose leaves of wanked-on women.

Mix with me, Pig Thief,
our *together* is better than theirs.

They belong to us, these After Woods. We're fused
by the death-trap seam,
welded together like cut-and-shut cars.

Feel my head, Pig Thief!
I'm as hot as a county tyre fire!
Feel my heart! The thrum
of an electric razor! And my brain
is throbbing like a juicy bone. The buzz off of me,
like jellies and e! A hum!
I'm sloshing like an egg in a leaky radiator!

The light pours out of me like Saint Theresa,
or an open fridge.

These are The After Woods. We will tell stories.

We will wear water. We will have gardens and draw water. Our
gardens will be made of stone. We will catch the water in pink
plastic tubs, ripped out from remodelled bathrooms in show-homes.
We will ride white horses over the rubble.

I'll be a fine lady.

When the world ends.

Pig Thief—

Here it comes again, the midday
depression settles like pesticide,
digging a splintery kiss from the mouth
doesn't help. I am okay, only
afternoons are hard, people are hard;
it's hard going out, getting things done . . .

      I should write it down. I should
      be able to write it down, but here
      is the blank page, full of a fine
      pedigree bulldog deafness. And here
      is my fitted wardrobe, a Last Chance Saloon
      of mid nineties knitwear. Here is my dog,
      little yellow usurper with a dressmaker's mouth.
      Here is my life, in all its non-refundable fire
      hazard motley. I cannot exactly say I am thrilled . . .

I am bored, boring. *Grief*
is very boring. Anger like this
is very boring. Who wants to be
Eibhlín Dubh Ní Chonaill, putting
on her *long loss* like a cardboard crown?
I want smithereen rages. I'm not
an own-goal Goldilocks, singing the blues.
I'm not! But I can't get it out, my poems
clump together in painful word wedgies,
make me ridiculous to myself. God,
this hardboiled habit forming fury.
It paralyses me. And my stupid accolade
patois, with tomahawk truculence, beaten back.
I want to say how abject-lovely you were.

But love is a lightbulb you put in your mouth,
and you can't take it out without breaking the glass . . .

Pig Thief—

Yes, I am talking to you. I am angry with *you*. Eibhlín isn't
angry. Eibhlín is an eighteenth century noblewoman. I am
not. I lack poise. I listen to The Smiths and snap gum, a pert,
partaking girl, swinging her hips in a ridge of sour lemon light.
You wouldn't catch Eibhlín down The Slimes, shock-headed
and sniffing physic. Saturday night, Gothed up for the colony
fondle. From high outside myself I watch my fingers flirt like
worms: pale partygoers, writhing. Eibhlín would know better.
This *process* lacks dignity. I am a gutless glass slipper. I am a
holdall for bones . . .

Wait, this was supposed to be about you, not just another peevish
confessional. I'm sorry, but you are hard to approach, writing you
~~is like staring into the sun~~ is staring into the sun. Let's talk about
you, all about you, your body in bodacious bloom, not one of the
quailing poor, but proper fierce. The day I took your picture, Pig
Thief sprawling shirtless like a flabbergasted Christ, or Pig Thief
à la Laura Palmer, wrapped in plastic, Caucasoid beneath the
conifers. There's Pig Thief, loaded and bony, cringing in a roadside
shrine, keeping the rain off his dreads. Pig Thief after Eastfield, that
look of depraved seraphic fatigue in the absolute zero unit of dawn,
making plans with sloppy gestures and degenerate cognition. Pig
Thief's face, a bruised bobbed apple floating in the bath. Pig Thief's
long neck, craned like the arm of a Metal Mickey. Pig Thief clinging
and clutching on me, the back end of a Pantomime horse . . .

Pig Thief—

You promised to hold me again,
to make me catch my breath
like a bomb scare.

Our loose flesh expelling air;
my slack squeezed tits are
whoopee cushions.

This isn't easy. I won't stay
young. Already I resemble
a rubber chicken,
an embarrassment of yellow skin.

You promised that you'd hold me,
make me tic like a tapped phone,
half daft in the sapping dark;
slippery and devout and getting slow,

You wouldn't want me now.
This needing aches. Pain
in its plentiful petticoat folds,
tight leafed as a head of lettuce,
sweet and crisp and plain and green . . .

Pig Thief—

I am gross with clacking melancholia, mad in the *auld stylee*. Today the sunshine is a decoy, two inadequate swans are bobbing. The weather is a Cheer-up Charlie. I want to punch God in the face. This feeling comes and goes, making my mouth do 'O's of moist resentment. Because he is out there, the man who made you dead. When I think about him I crumple up like paper money, stuttering, buffering, a slow modem stretching my words. He can come and go as he pleases, strutting his clubland stuff, hedging his vengeance with pleasure, coked to the eyeteeth and reeling to the righteous rhythm of his hitman's jitters. Violence has made him a minor celebrity. Antihero, all matinee swank. He's a million True Crime dramas: gold teeth and abnormally juicy wounds . . .

The warm air sucks me like a bagless vacuum. I rock my low level longing. I wish I could picture you, sleepy as a storybook prince, jugged in the earth. Instead I have my panicked slapstick, saying your name, seeing that man, I'm sweaty and shrink-wrapped in ugly blue sheets . . .

A coherent scattering: Mystic, the prodigal, returns to Ireland. From her Journal.

Flight often thinks of the dead.
It's in the abrasion. The light
eats the air like an apple. I creep
in the cabin's sucked marrow; pluck
a honeysuck dangle of oxygen,
an orange, an orchid; close my eyes, or type.

At this height I'm always mistaking
distance for symmetry, a coherent
scattering of houses and lawns.

But if Dublin is waiting, she doesn't let on.
Not indifferent, just *preoccupied*.
She leaves it to flight to think of you:

a thought, braced between
the blue headrests, the chemical
crapper and the jumbo peanuts,
all this stuff in Schrödinger limbo.

Dublin doesn't know that I hold
onto a thirst so sharp it could skin shit.
She is busy with motorways.

And when I walk out of terminal two,
without a cigarette or spare
change or coffee, I will forget.

I'll make an abstinence of morning,
go hungry, feeling vaguely
travel sick.

I'll wait for a bus into town,

watching the daylight kick
contrails out of the way
like untidy electrical cable.

We will be a nativity: Mystic writes to Pig Thief's brother to arrange a meeting.

DECEMBER 11TH, 2009   STONEYBATTER.

Frankie—

You will meet me, won't you?
I have flowers for your garden.
We always try to borrow life from living things.
It is our way. But you have children now. I am glad
you didn't name them after us. They'll hear other
words for what they are. For fuck's sake, teach them
no history. History's what The Dead have in lieu of religion.
They pin their deadness to their chest like holy medals. Who
wants that? That's not for kids.

Come over. Bring Nana and Kathleen and the boys.
I have been writing a song. We will be a nativity,
gathered together under a sloping roof. A line of amber
lights will guide us to the wet relishing of drink.

An indecency of darkness: Mystic writes to Pig Thief on her return, remembering their time together, inviting an invocation.

Pig Thief—

These walls have no ears, or eyes or lips. They are brick. Heavy and immobile as the thickset features of rural policemen. Who is counting, if this is the fifth or the fifty-fifth time I am telling? I have pulled back the peeling paper and toilet-stall-scribbled myself in the past: *I woz 'ere, 'ere I woz.* This will be an accounting. Nobody asks *you* to remember. So *I* am asking. Squint through the sun like the sun was a keyhole and see, see us, see me and the lads; see your jug-eared brother and his short blonde wife. We let the weather talk us into pubs. Drinking is scratching a thing in wax. A barroom snug is a black box recorder. This will be a retelling.

Look: here are cells, here are scaffolds, here are caravans. Here is you, aswim, and me. The women are reservoirs here, mothers are full of fish, of us. Here is your Grandfather's fist, a clan gavel banged in the aching face. Here are the scatterbrained heatwaves, here are the stars, spotted above the unemployment blackspots. *This* is The Long Ago, Life of Lives. You should know how it goes, how we jaunted out of the country, breathing typhus and fornication, landed on the city's shot glass rim. When we clasped our hands together and prayed, they said, we looked like flies frenziedly rubbing their forelegs together.

Everything changes. Now it's all marble sinks and US crime drama. Batmobile cars and kerbside shit. Border towns puffed up like unplanned pregnancies, gaudy with all the elective surgeries of urban renewal. It's pricey and garish, a gift shop at an amusement park, and everything must go: buy Bono buy crack buy Guinness and Chunky Kit-Kats buy Mary coy as a centrefold buy boxes of bones and imperfect contrition buy cappuccino and Bram Stoker

buy Synge and O'Casey buy collateral damage and clan tartan buy
Bono and pro-life bigotry buy golf clubs buy a deep fried gristle
of chicken buy shamrock trackies, tax dodges and Bono buy
Bloomsday and Bono buy the fug of gum disease and Bono and
the GPO and Bono and dossers and Bono and exchange students,
gimcrack Yanks and Bono.

They will not buy you. I am renaming the cities and towns with a
childish pique. I'm misdirecting so they'll never know, never find
you find us find here. Only I will go, and I will travel this telling.
Remember, Pig Thief, follow.

I will walk through crime families and cage fights. I will walk along
tramlines, crossed divining rods, dousing impersonal tonnage
of steel. I will walk the truant afternoons, double daring, egging
you on. I will walk the chickenshit squeal of breaks. I will walk
an indecency of darkness, Pig Thief, picked out by headlights,
goofing beside the power lines. You will walk with me, and your
arched back will resemble the harp, Your pale bleed of hair. You're
pale, wane of face. Your father, you claim, is a Sweeney, sweating
his madness in a Limerick safe house. The thorny joy of going to
extremes! You will walk beside me, we will play Blood or Whiskey
/ The Cranberries. Talk about Meinhof / Zapata / Buddha. Cod
gurus kidding ourselves, in love with our own potluck learning. The
stalwart horseplay of fucking! You, in the hallucinated dawn before
dying. The spread of my thighs: scenic gateway to the sagging south.
You will remember.

You will remember cider and The Dead. I am still, rehearsing the
shape of my coffin. The cemetery wears an allowance of black, an
artillery of stars. I lie back in an obsolescence of roses and watch
the light turn to powder. I am not afraid. I'm full of the bluesy *soon*
of coming. Give me little lathing kisses. Give me birds buoyed up
above the public library, or rice white over the quays, testing their
wings on the water. Give me oil in my lamp, keep me burning. But

Pig Thief, hammered, banjaxed, dead on his flat-footed doggerel, slurring, a warm blooded punk who feels the pricking of his thumbs and says he has to go. Walk this with me. Walk a night shot through with white creases like scuffed leather. Remember. Pig Thief, gone into glue-fume and combat, gone into the bungalow lands, their stone cladding and druggy gums. Pig Thief, hawking hens' teeth in tarmacked parks, bagging an endless crematoria of coke. Pig Thief doing alchemy, combustion of blood / premonition / smoke / huff / freebase / remember. Cider and The Dead. Reading you Joyce, rendering love like ritual fat. I skim little lip smacks, fall back onto shivs of bright green gravel. I am gutted.

I will walk the fairgrounds. Carousel horses painted like churches. Girls as lurid as headache-saints. The friction and the fastness! The kinetics of sex: grease / steam / longing. Your body, wet and hot, bare foot inside a leather sandal, rubs me raw. My heart is a filled blister, so sore. We call this *memory, biography, those were the days*. Remember: we saw that skinny white horse go by, a schizoid jinx, rolling its yellow eye, pulling a tarped cart full of stolen scrap. You grabbed my hand. Traffic talking to the bruised bronze hearts of the monuments. Skinny white horse, weaving through cars. It was Death that was coming. We did not know. I am reading Joyce again, twisting my hungers until they squeak like balloons. You have the wide eyed look of the doomed. That Phonecian mask replacing your face. Stilldark, star sparse mornings, city sucking blood from its cut up knuckle. The first brood of grief. Flexing Flatrock like a muscle. Holiday. A cold grey hour. Jetlag. April. Ireland. May. I forget where I'm going. Guide me.

Nobody asks *you* to remember. So *I* am asking. That last time, standing in Spar, dazed by the shop-lifting light. Walked backwards out of our Kell Chronology to here. Come here, to this, wearing the flayed skins of our enemies: combat boots and khaki trousers. I waited for you to buy Guinness. I waited for you to buy crack buy Bono buy chunky Kit-Kats buy stars to snort by the chimneyful. I waited for you to buy heroin buy postcards buy heroes buy dead buy Bono and mauve smoke and jaundiced shrieking. Dead are ticketed, toe-tagged on velvet. You wanted it / them / this. *A linking up*, you said. I watch your pockets get lighter, buying Starbucks and page three and Bono buying Saint Rita Saint Jude and Bono buying showband bodies and Bono and full-English breakfasts and theme pubs and ~~Bono~~

Pig Thief, see the Millwall wail of my open mouth: *what has this got to do with us?* Stuff a corpse with sawdust, prop it up, flog it off, give it a crown or a conical cap. So what? See me say how I want to go home, talk about Meinhof / O'Connell / Spare. Undress in a clean extremity of silence. Compliance of kisses, calm / numb / an adequate flatline.

There's a ribbon for the words to run on: a gag, a black blindfold, a black Scalextric track. Clever machine. I'm forcing the forceps torsion of words *out!* through their hammer blows: *This paper is a shrine to striking. This paper is a shrine to striking!* We wanted something better but neither of us knew how. It's as simple as that. An old joke about *culture* and *mould*. Here they come now to buy us back, a rugby scrum of tourist tat. Here are the cars with tinted windows, tinny speakers, dead boys and Bono. Here is the crew from Channel 4. Here are the hipsters with flowers in their hair, who don't understand, not even stray dogs choose this freedom. Here is a life, a fire-consignment.

To The Mystic from the Pig Thief:
January 2010

My Mystic—

These, my dreams, are footage of falling. I am falling through you. I can see everything now: Ireland, slouchy and stark mad, maligned hardloving towns of worthy filth. I see the Old Man, whose face is fossil record, cotton mouthing shots of black Sambuca. I see Big Jim's boys, handgun gobshites, arrogant with pain. I see the girls, done up with desolate golden croissants for hair, strung out on jettison-techno, doing flirty trance in different colours, arms raised up and preening at the sky going *fuck the pain away.* I can see you. I am you. I am the words in your mouth, garbled in comedown. I can see everything: Ulster, a bimbo Lady Macbeth, scrubbing her red hand madly; a lank frieze of bodies, glum with blood, packing their bleak fineries. I see the heat has jammy mouthparts, the morning going on and on like an autobahn, taking an age for the sun to rise. I see the soft rock ruin of the dockyard. I see the living, see the Faithful Departed: spastic phantoms who have hugged our ceilings like balloons. And I see myself, as cheekbone decently dead as any boyband apology for *dissident* can be. Don't cry, Biddy, I was a real suave trendsetting corpse.

Being dead isn't how you'd think. It changes you. I'm going through my figurings out, all my unbecomings. I been a crow flower, disinfected with sunlight strong as sheep dip. I been yellow and white, institutional and flamboyant. I come up all pert and poking at The Holy Child Church. I dossed the dank, weedy dirt beds down by the railway station, nodding my perking princeling head. After that I was a dog for a bit. I snicker-snacked fat rabbits, drank out of puddles, scratched my spine along the rusty railings. Then I was a bird. Flight is a form of language, you said. I was writing *Pomana!* with my wings, yeah? It's like pissing your name in the snow. It doesn't last, so I put on my hunger like a coat and gone into the wild, slashed-up scabby black of the pines. I gone up in the branches, packing them out with the snow. I saw a Hunter's Moon, misshapen as a hornet's nest. I couldn't stop staring, and someone was ringing the Angelus. I got dizzy, get dizzy, so drunk you could pour me in a fucking bowl, so drunk that thinking is liquid. Witless shitfaced *wunderkind*, me! The sky drowned in its own weightlessness. It was all bare and insufferable bright. I saw your hair lying on the lake like smoke on a mirror, spreading itself through the water in loose dissolving treacle coils. I spoke to it. I was sounding the depths of it. It didn't speak back. I lie in its damp bracket and sleep.

I went on to be a star then, or I was a sound, or I was one of them other small, intense majesties. You catch on fast how many deaths there are. It's amazing we get the right ones. Somebody somewhere is taking great care. That thought should give you comfort, but I know it won't.

But that's how I come here. It's just a place, nothing fancy, kind of cool and silver like an old zinc bath, like a caravan. Hey, I'm back where I started! Did I say, your hair's grown long, Biddy? I'm laddering up it at night. It's thick and brittle and it never smelled so clean.

It wasn't my fault, you know. Hate is a hard husbandry. I wasn't sharp enough 'cause I didn't care enough. I couldn't take it seriously, all their pent lethality. I try to feel sorry about it, but I don't. We don't get guilt, I guess, the dead, we get *flower* and *bird* and *dog* and *star*; *wind* and *sound* and *stone* instead. And I get Flatrock too, maybe. Flatrock until God's speed ends and the sun splits the stones, till somebody puts the bitch-slapped sparkle of the stars out of our misery. Flatrock until forever, Biddy. You too, in the finish.

You mustn't be scared. This dying comes on as a hot pink light so bright it's sharp. It dazzles, makes you glow, a UV strobing at a rave. Grows you like weed in a greenhouse. Then there's nothing else to know. You feel Faradised! You feel Teslaed! It's mad! Me, streaming with the sickly heat of a Falaraki suntan! Me, like a Three Mile Island. It buzz me, Biddy.

I'm not like you, I cannot do the follow-on of things, join up all our horrors like a kiddie linking daisies. For me there is only the super colliding fire of the next near moment. I am no *Recording Angel*. You write it, the raw smear of History. You write it, with the received wisdom of a rear window. You make it matter, if you can. But understand, it don't contain me, it evolves me, breathing me out to my becoming Flatrock. You can't hold a ghost like hash in the lungs. I don't mean to hurt you, you just can't. Trust me, I can see everything now: the future styling its sympathetic wounds. There's smell of smoke in the hard cold air, hanging a sentence over the safehouse.

Notes

Flatrock, Northern Ireland is a cipher. Nowhere of that name exists.

Pomana is a cyclically recurring meal, held in honour of a person who has died.

Eibhlín Dubh Ní Chonaill was an eighteenth century noblewoman and poet. She wrote the long poem *Lament for Art Ó Laoghaire* after her husband's murder, mourning him and calling for revenge.

Lightning Source UK Ltd.
Milton Keynes UK
UKOW04f0707171115

262908UK00003B/96/P